Learning to Manage Our Fears

Learning to Manage Our Fears

JAMES W. ANGELL

Abingdon / Nashville

LEARNING TO MANAGE OUR FEARS

Library of Congress Cataloging in Publication Data

ANGELL, JAMES W.
  Learning to manage our fears.
  1. Fear. I. Title.
  BF575.F2A48   248.'4   81-1878   AACR2

ISBN 0-687-21329-0

Scripture quotations unless otherwise noted are from the Revised
Standard Version of the Bible, copyrighted 1946, 1952, 1971, © 1973, by
the Division of Christian Education of the National Council of the
Churches of Christ in the U.S.A., and used by permission. Those noted
NEB are from The New English Bible. © the Delegates of the Oxford
University Press and the Syndics of the Cambridge University Press
1961, 1970. Reprinted by permission. Those noted JB are from The
Jerusalem Bible, copyright © 1966 by Darton, Longman & Todd, Ltd.,
and Doubleday & Company, Inc. Used by permission of the publisher.
Those noted Phillips are from The New Testament in Modern English,
copyright © J. B. Phillips 1958, 1960, 1972.

Poem on page 28 is reprinted by permission of the author.

Prayer on page 69 is from *Prayers* by Michel Quoist © Sheed & Ward Inc.
(now Andrews & McMeel Inc.), 1963. All rights reserved. Reprinted by
permission.

Excerpt on pages 73-75 is from the December 1961 *McCall's*, © 1961 by
the McCall Corporation. Used with permission of the McCall Publishing
Company.

MANUFACTURED BY THE PARTHENON PRESS AT
NASHVILLE, TENNESSEE, UNITED STATES OF AMERICA

Contents

Like the eagle, . . . your nest is
set among the stars.

—Obadiah 1:4

Introduction

The earth is approximately 3,400 million years old. If you reduced its age to a century, Homo sapiens showed up just minutes ago. But a lot has happened since that first big bang, or whatever awesome impulse set this magnificent process in motion.

Language and libraries, laws and love have made civilization possible. Electricity has been grabbed from the sky. Caves have been exchanged for cities, stone tools traded for steel ones. Dances around campfires have been replaced by a dance of electrons on oscilloscopes, and Jupiter has been photographed up close.

Some things, though, stand unchanged: the restless white wind, blue and green splashes of sea; sun, flowers, trees, rain; autumn flights of birds; light, darkness, birth, death. The precise spin of the rhinestone pieces of heaven.

And the omnipresence of fear.

Good old fear. Almost as old as God. As Alfred-

Hitchcock scary as a squeaking step of a haunted house at midnight. As much at home among primordial man and monsters as among siloed missiles, dead-aimed from somewhere at the pleasant street on which I live.

The pages that follow have something to say about fear—how we can learn to live with it, understand it, laugh at it, utilize it, and, by the power of living faith, come at last to raise a tattered victor's flag over its remembered ruins.

I'm a minister, one of whose jobs is to talk about fear—and faith. To walk into a pulpit on a regular basis and try to respond to the question, Is there any word from the Lord?

Congregations are hard to fool. They know the difference between someone who has something to say and someone who must say something. Most preachers admit to having done both on occasion.

Fortunately, most congregations are generous enough to put up with a good bit of theological blabbing if now and then a little real news breaks through. I'm privileged to serve a fine group of people, and my prayer is that there are at least some days when they don't go home disappointed.

One of my surest impressions of the pulpit is that whenever I have tried to talk about fear—about what can be done to manage it, tame it, or blow it out of the water—person after person greeting me afterward has said, "Today you were talking to me." I hope this book talks to you.

The Winner and Still Champion— The Fears We Have About Ourselves

> Don't get exercised over nameless faces and faceless enemies. Accept your fears and worries. Some of them are legitimate, but most of them are imagined and needless. Know the difference. Know what to fear.
>
> —Donald Shelby

You can't afford to be afraid. None of us can.

Along a certain street I regularly travel is a business that deals in building supplies. On its lot are the usual stacks of lumber, triangular mounds of sand, crushed rock, and bricks creating the effect of a small Navaho village, silver coils of fencing, concrete benches and birdbaths.

Driving down that street recently, I also noticed, on the company's changeable letter sign, just below the company name, a special offer. It read: "Stepping Stones: 10 percent off." Always on the prowl for ideas, I was fascinated by the various facets of meaning the offer appeared to suggest.

Discounts are inviting, but *stepping stones*? I felt a suspicion that there may be a number of experiential stepping stones on which it's impossible to reduce the price: trust born of experience, faith paid for by suffering, victories that demand vast quantities of patience and courage.

A few blocks later I noticed another sign: "Deadbolts Installed Within Eight Hours of Your Order." With this advertisement the subtlety was gone. We are a locked-up, locked-in, scared generation.

An evening walk, in many urban areas at least, is a thing of the past. Double-digit inflation means most families live in fear the money won't stretch. Parents worry about things that might happen to their kids. Kids worry about aging parents. Everybody worries about a nuclear war.

"Down deep," a friend of mine said recently, "I'm scared to death." And, when I took this manuscript to an editor, his first comment was, "My wife needs this book." But persons willing to trust God also have achieved some clarity about things they are *not* afraid of.

Fear is a robber. A dirty crook. A rip-off artist, lying in ambush.

Yet fear is something else, too. It's a lifesaving emotional asset. It's rent we pay for the chance to live on life's growing edge. It's a warning system with a purpose, a testing system of the quality of our courage, a creative force at work in our daily lives.

Henry Ward Beecher once called fear "a kind of bell or gong which rings the mind into quick life and avoidance on the approach of danger." It's also part of the chemistry out of which excellence is often born. A fear of tyranny created the United States of America.

Somewhere along the road of yesterday was a James Cagney film entitled *Man of a Thousand Faces*. Fear can match that.

We live with myriad fears. Fear of rejection, of failure, of pain; the fear of dying. Of the possibility that God is a fiction or that life is a farce. We are afraid of the unknown, of becoming pregnant, or of growing old and helpless. Of being robbed, hurt, or seeing someone else hurt. Of bankruptcy or a plunging stock market, being unloved, or loving someone too much. Being discovered. Not being discovered. Strangers. Elevators. Mistakes. Street gangs. Rats. Earthquakes. Blood. Or bill collectors at the door.

We freeze at the sound of a siren or telephone call in the night. We are afraid of being betrayed, losing our marbles, not being able to find a job, becoming addicted. The Russians, emptiness, loneliness, anger, cancer, radioactive poisoning, lack of oil. Of giving a speech. Flying. Flunking an exam. The fast flow of time.

Fear can erupt into a Mt. St. Helens, but more often it simply wears away happiness and personal peace like the tread of a tire, leaving the surface of our lives bare and hard.

It's not correct to say that fear can be overcome. Fear cannot and should not be banished from the

13

universe. A world without anxiety would be a flat, dishonest world, a world without passion or surprise. And we don't want that. Fear can't be permanently conquered and left for dead, but it *can* be unmasked, disarmed, and denied a victory of its own, or converted into a form of confidence.

There is, indeed, a positive side to fear.

A favorite story told of legendary-and-notably-tough football coach Paul Bryant has to do with one of his players who, in a race down the field in the midst of a big game, overtook an opponent about to score, even though the man with the ball was known to be a faster runner.

Asked to explain his exceptional performance, Bryant's defense player described the fear that turned him into a winner, "That guy was running for a touchdown," he said, "but I was running for my life!"

Among God's many fascinating kinds of gifts is adrenalin. Fear can multiply our strength in emergencies, and there are thousands of case studies to prove it. I'm not sure we are *always* given all the genius or stamina of soul a situation may demand. If that were so, there would be no suicides. But what is beyond question is that, as kites rise before the wind, danger and trouble frequently prompt us to find and utilize emotional reserves that we never knew were there until a crisis called them into play.

Of the million things we are capable of being afraid of—handguns, war, silence, floods, ghosts—we still have no trouble crowning the winner of the derby. We're most afraid of whatever challenges or undermines our self-worth.

We're most afraid:

—other people will think we're not attractive

—that we appear ugly or stupid

—that we haven't been successful compared to others

—that we're young and naïve, or old and uninteresting—not of much use to society or,

—that we're not sexually capable, or are sexually obsessed

—that God doesn't approve of us, and has good reason not to.

A certain amount of skepticism about our adequacy is normal. No one "makes it" on all points of the coping compass. But faith tells us that God believes in us, and that this becomes a basis for believing in ourselves.

Our affirmation *of one another* is also part of the conquest of self-doubt, especially if "I love you" is taken to mean "I *believe* in you."

The opposite of fear may be stoic bravery. More often it's relaxed love.

Some of the wisest words ever spoken to me about my job were these: "You can stand in the pulpit and say, 'I love you,' 'I love you,' 'I love you,' but if you do not *really* love the people to whom those words are addressed, they will come out: 'I hate you,' 'I hate you,' 'I hate you.' And, conversely, if your love of those who are listening is authentic, you can say, 'I hate you,' 'I hate you,' 'I hate you,' and it will come out: 'I love you,' 'I love you,' 'I love you.'"

To take the offensive against fear may also include the decision to risk some transient embarrassment for entrance into a street called Freedom, or a house called Self. To risk being real is to learn new things about ourselves. With risking, paranoia can lift like a fog before a warming sun.

To risk some mistakes is also to gain fresh information about our ability to feel. It's become intellectually popular of late to make fun of feeling—as if it were one of the discredited pastimes of the Sixties. Yet, in an increasingly technologically managed, privacy-conscious society, the ability to feel may be one of our most crucial "lost horizons."

Dr. Roy Menninger, psychiatrist, warned an audience of executives against the substitution of achievement for feeling. By idolizing prestige and immersing themselves in environments that stress results, Menninger said, many wind up believing "it is what they do, not what they feel, that makes them real, and that if they couldn't do those things no one would look up to them.

"Some never become aware of the fallacy of such thinking," he said. "Others are saved—by a divorce or a heart attack at age 44—by being forced to ask themselves where their values really lie." Most of those listening acknowledged, in later conversations, that they had no one to talk to.

It wasn't that there was no one to listen, but there

16

was a dam that made one-half of a person a stranger to the other.

The famous physician-counselor went on to say that this isn't just a manager's disease. "Many people," he added, "don't recognize the feelings of anger, depression, grief and are not in touch with themselves."

Fear again. Nameless and numbing.

Social conditioning tells us that it's bad to fail, that it hurts to be laughed at, that nice people don't say bad things. So, we end up with layers of asbestos between our deep inner worlds and our outward actions—between one set of impressions we think we are making and another that we are.

Unless we are in touch with our feelings, we will watch the world through windows that resemble the bottom of cold drink bottles.

In orientation sessions with couples planning to be married, I sometimes ask prospective brides and grooms if they know what the other is most afraid of. Most don't. That's not easy to answer.

Often we can't reveal feelings that ebb and flow within us because even we do not accurately recognize them. Or we bury feelings that threaten to cause pain, such as sorrow. Yet the apostle Paul tells us: "There is nothing love cannot face" (I Cor. 13:7a NEB).

A persistent question from childhood is, *What are you going to be when you grow up?* How often that's asked. Are you going to be a farmer? A teacher? A doctor? An engineer? At one point I was sure I wanted to be a Greyhound bus driver!

Dr. William Glasser says a new question overtook that one, about 1950. It was, *Who* are you going to be?

To be cataloged as a banker, salesperson, scientist, or race car driver was not, we came to understand, the most important thing to be said about a human being. Vocation still isn't the most important decision each of us must make about either the future or the present.

A better question is, How *aware* will I be? How *alive*? How *concerned* about others? By what *faith* and *values* will I live? By what or whose *dreams*? And, by what measure will I measure my worth— especially by what measurements that have nothing whatsoever to do with money?

Fear flowing out of such concerns is worth welcoming and wanting.

In the first days of the Revolution when Aaron Burr was a young man, not yet involved in the military or the government, he and a girl friend, Dolly Quincy, were in a small crowd in Litchfield, Massachusetts, one afternoon, listening to firsthand reports from a soldier who had escaped British-held Boston. Burr, who would later become famous in our history for other reasons, said of this first sampling of war: "This fellow claimed to have been at Lexington. I am sure he gave us many bloody details, but I no longer recall a word he said. I do remember daffodils in bloom—a goose and goslings gliding across the still, cold water of a pond."

Governments change. The donkey cart is replaced by the steam engine. Waterpower by electric power. Airplanes by space capsules. DuPont and Madison Avenue continue to design and draw us into marvelous new worlds of convenience. Other pieces of the human equation change shape and color. But all this still leaves, in its wake, perennial essences such as two people in love and goslings on a pond. Plus the story of a bush on fire, or a Voice from heaven saying, "This is my beloved Son . . . listen to him" (Matt. 17:5).

So we live, suspended out among the Starkeeper's stars, and a million uncertainties suggested by the tune "What's It All About, Alfie?" There are uncountable things that *could* happen. Yet against this myriad of contingencies, and a threat of nothingness there stands a Sovereign Love and a promise.

If we can become convinced that these are not softheaded fictions but the most important truths we possess, the future will be filled, not with nightmares, but with songs.

Did You Miss
Your Big Chance—
Or Just Imagine That
You Did?

This could but have happened once,
And we missed it, lost it forever.
—Robert Browning, *Youth and Art*

Every evening about sunset, at a popular resort hotel on Maui, a young Hawaiian walks to the edge of a nearby precipice, looks thoughtfully for a moment at the orange sky, then dives into the warm, blue Pacific waters below.

It is ritual, and dinner guests on the terrace anticipate the moment: the mysterious magic of twilight, the link with the past, the gracefully silhouetted brown body, plunging a hundred feet into the sea.

There is no announcement. It simply happens about the time torches are being lighted about the grounds to add more glamour to the evening. You have to be alert, or you could miss it.

A friend of mine did.

"I just turned around to say something to Marge," she told me, "and I *missed* it. Darn it!"

Many people, both at the conscious and unconscious level, have the same feeling about life. Something crucial didn't occur. If it did, they were in the wrong place at the right time or in the right place at the wrong time.

The big promotion never came. The recognition that would have said, "You made it! Welcome to Club Success," never occurred. A deferred adventure disappeared into oblivion, lost in what Gail Sheehy calls the "apostrophe in time between the end of growing up and the beginning of growing old." A marriage made in heaven wound up going down the tubes. Boredom with making money, and a running after prizes which, once possessed, became in retrospect a project closer to vanity than to victory.

Now it's too late.

This is common experience for men for whom our cultural expectations in the past have been so high, for whom our macho checklist for having "made it" have been so well defined and agreed upon.

Women now can look forward, in their liberation, to a similar post–thirty-five rendezvous with, "Did I, or didn't I?"

As long as I've been talking with people about the demand for meaning, I've been haunted by these lines:

Life is not lost by dying! Life is lost
Minute by minute, day by dragging day,
In all the thousand, small uncaring ways.

The fear of wasting our chance also may be our
deliverance. That kind of fear isn't pathological; it is
disguised blessing. It can enable us to keep our
expectations high and fuel our determination not to
miss the dive off Black Rock into the Pacific.

One of the best-known stages of disillusion, or
dismay at not having accomplished more than the
record seems to show, is the forties. The vice-
presidency, if it were ever coming, would be here by
now. Marriage for the most part has been demystified
and looks as if it will be but more of what already has
been. Health, wealth, friends, the future—all starts to
look fixed.

But, like some of our finest poets who died with
their work still unpublished, most of us cannot know
and will never know what we have contributed to life
that will last.

If we're going to talk about dreams that didn't
quite make it, let me share a few of mine.

The first involved the college from which I was
graduated in 1941.

The summer day I enrolled, my parents were with
me and, because the office of the dean of admissions
was being redecorated, we met for the signing of the
registration forms in an adjoining office—the office
of the president.

President Harper was on vacation and the campus

seemed semideserted, so the dean ushered the three of us into the executive quarters and invited me to sit in the president's high-backed leather chair to fill out the application. With a twinkle in his eye he said, "Who knows—maybe some day *you'll* be president!" My dad and mother grinned.

Thirty years later my name showed up on a list of possible candidates to fill the office. My experience had been mostly in religion rather than education, but I also had training as a lawyer and thought I could handle the job. I remembered my registration-day experience. But the college found someone better qualified.

Later came a race for General Assembly Moderator, the highest elective office of our denomination. Ordinarily two or three persons are endorsed and the Assembly chooses one but, in 1974, seven of us wound up on the platform describing how we would try to move the church forward under our leadership.

Losing didn't hurt that much. Still, it was another ambition denied.

A third round of "capture the flag" involved the possibility that I might be called to a pastorate in Washington, D.C., wind up successor to Dr. Peter Marshall at the New York Avenue Presbyterian Church. For a year the possibility hung in the air. There were interviews, exchanges of correspondence, hints of something big to happen. Then, one day, word came that the Washington decision had been made. Someone else would be going there.

For every disappointment I have known, though,

thirty-six fabulous other things have excited my existence and started a music in the treetops of my soul.

Life's real wins often come in secret garb. What looked wasted, like a young man's death in a Jerusalem suburb, turns out to constitute the salvation of the world.

No, we can't really measure the lasting contributions of our lives, which Peter Marshall called their "donation" in contrast to their duration. Only God can do that. And the idea of crossing an imagined boundary, which means, "If you haven't made it by now, you never will," is wrong. Pablo Casals and Winston Churchill are only two of thousands for whom life had its chief significance, not after age forty but after sixty.

An enduring marriage and well-paying job were once all the proof that seemed to be needed to show that we had our act together—that life was unfolding on cue. Other forms of success were nice, but not necessary. Persons tended to settle for one marriage, one career, one ride on the merry-go-round. But 1984 came early and today we have an opportunity to live several lifetimes, each capable of being important at its own time and in its own way.

As for marriage, it's still a vivid, suspenseful chapter, but no longer the total book. Nor are dissolutions of marriage the stigmatizing disasters they once were thought to be. Dignity has been reasserted for singleness.

And after-age-fifty surprises and contributions are now expected to be as numerous as those before.

But as life has become more and more crowded with options, so are our fears multiplied and harder to deal with. Yesterday it was premature death by smallpox or diphtheria. Today it's the thought that life may be uselessly prolonged by a vacuum pump.

Yesterday it was a dust bowl and a shortage of dollars. Today it's the possibility of planetary contamination and mass starvation.

Yesterday it was the embarrassment of an unmarried girl becoming pregnant, leaving to visit her aunt in a neighboring town for a while. Today it's moral ambivalence over tens of thousands of public-financed abortions.

We've become grafted into the larger dilemmas of humankind whether we wanted to be or not and our fears have been upsized in the process. The spinoff is that we now also have a chance to compound our compassion and be, not only poetically, but also literally, one with all humankind.

Each day brings choices, sometimes of unusual consequence to others, sometimes of special significance to us. There's an unexpected knock on the door or a voice at the other end of a telephone wire. Or a letter drops through the mail slot and the universe reels.

Shakespeare said we are actors. That means each and every day is another opening night. And life, in the words of an introduction Ray Bradbury once inserted in front of one of his plays, is for performance by "any glad company of fools." So we go on practicing our lines, doing our comedy, dying onstage at the matinee, making another entry at 8 P.M.

In the final part of the Sermon on the Mount Jesus describes what I call the sin of average living. He says that if we do only what others do—if we love only those who love us in return, in what way can our life be said to be any different? Here, perhaps, are hints of the real chances we don't want to pass by.

Sigmund Freud said we need to love deeply and hate wisely. Anyone who can do that doesn't need to lie awake at night brooding over the possibility of having lived a failed life.

There's a story about an overseer of a home for children who was upset about a girl who lived there. She was unattractive and had mannerisms that made the superintendent want to get rid of her. Other youngsters seemed to fit into the foster home environment, but she was a mess. He reasoned that if some way could be found to have her transferred to another institution, one established especially for delinquents, his own operation would be fine.

One day he looked out a window and saw her pinning a note to a tree. Imagining she was up to one more mischief and that this might be precisely the evidence he needed to have her transferred, he ran out, grabbed the note, and read it. In awkwardly printed letters it said: "Whoever Finds This Note, I Love You."

The fear we may miss the brass ring—never really get our act together—has its answer in the confidence that comes to us from that Galilean who said "The kingdom of God cometh not with observation" (Luke 17:20 KJV).

And, though the following tabulation of prayers that seemed not to be answered, yet strangely were, has been quoted many times, it still sounds a glorious chord of encouragement:

> I asked God for strength, that I might achieve,
> I was made weak, that I might learn humbly to obey . . .
> I asked for health, that I might do greater things,
> I was given infirmity, that I might do better things . . .
> I asked for riches, that I might be happy,
> I was given poverty, that I might be wise . . .
> I asked for power, that I might have the praise of men,
> I was given weakness, that I might feel the need of God . . .
> I asked for all things, that I might enjoy life,
> I was given life, that I might enjoy all things . . .
> I got nothing that I asked for—but everything I had hoped for,
> Almost despite myself, my unspoken prayers were answered.
> I am among all men, most richly blessed.

I once emceed in a children's TV show where I asked a group of eight-year-olds to play a word association game. I began with some simple words like "fun," "baseball," and "school." Then, when I said, "God," they answered with synonyms like "sky," "love," "big," "mountains," "creations," and, of course, "Jesus." But Alvin didn't say a thing.

"Alvin," I said, "what do you think of when I say God?"

Smiling, beneath his black curls, he replied, "People!"

A hug at a bus station. A late-night conversation after a date. Graduation memories. The trusted advice of a physician. The loyalty of friends. Sacrifices. These are the things time and faltering memories manage never to lose. They are the bicycles of the heart that can't be stolen.

In the midst of such moments, God is filling our spiritual emptiness and arming us against the invasions of fear.

We meet the Lord of human anxiety when the Bible falls open and we read about sea storms and crucifixions. But we meet him just as persuasively in the manifold touchings of our own experience that we have only started to name—touchings that make God's love tactile, prayer natural, faith in meaning undeniable.

Robert Hale reminds us how easy it is to forget:

Fear creeps in like a poisonous fog,
    making us pull down the shades
        and double-lock the doors.
Fear erects barriers of the mind
    more real than barbed wire
        or the Berlin Wall.
Trembling disciples behind our barricades of fear,
    we have forgotten the Master
        who walked through all barriers.

Whether that kind of faith begins with God and ends with people or begins with people and ends with God, I'm not sure. I am sure that herein lies an explanation of what freedom, love, dignity, and value are all about.

Converting Failures

> We must not let fear overleap its purpose into pathological manifestations. We must make it a friend, let it lead us to repentance, spur us to righteousness and redemption. We must see God working in our fear.
> —J. Wallace Hamilton, *Ride the Wild Horses!*

In an upper-south country cemetery there's a granite marker with these words engraved below the name of the deceased: "His Life Was a Failure: He Died Without Money."

That seems unfair.

Success, we've said, can't be measured by money. Ghandi's assets totaled $46 at the time of his death; Martin Luther King, Jr.'s, around $10,000.

Besides, who's to say?

History is cluttered with stories of the penniless and the disgraced, the momentarily forgotten and outrightly rejected who, long after their deaths, are finally identified as those most worthy to be remembered.

There's comfort in knowing today's failures may be tomorrow's heroes, but that possibility still doesn't do much to reduce the feeling we have when we have "bombed." Some great moment came and went, and left us behind choking on fumes and dust.

"I blew it!"

"We regret to inform you—."

"F."

"Better luck next time."

"Where's my name? It wasn't called."

In high school I lacked the size and talent to excel in athletics. So I tackled public speaking and, in both my sophomore and junior years, managed to win a silver medal in the declamatory contest. Earl B. won the gold.

Earl B. was a class ahead, so by the time I became a senior he was graduated and gone. Now I was almost certain to win first prize.

But James M., a transfer student, moved into town in September during the last term, entered the competition, and won it walking away.

Imagined failure is just as hurtful as real failure, especially if it involves an apparent inability to rise to the expectations of a family image.

Children of the famous have a tough time claiming their identities. Pierre Salinger's son, Marc, leaped to an early death from the Golden Gate Bridge. Los Angeles Mayor Tom Bradley's daughter has been arrested for shoplifting for the third time.

Faith has important things to say about failure. Its highest truth, the resurrection, began with a murder. The church has been buried a dozen times, but the "Light shines in the darkness, and the darkness has not overcome it" (John 1:5).

Faith, though, isn't doctrinal orthodoxy. It's closer to the "I-Thou" relationship Martin Buber wrote about and, like the biblical manna, calls for constant renewal and replenishment.

Dr. Frederick Speakman in *Love Is Something You Do* (Fleming H. Revell, 1959) described Christianity as a whole lifetime of fresh starts. He grew up in a small town in Ohio—a town with the courthouse in the middle, fringed by a pool hall, drugstore, post office, general store, and a musty lawyer's office. In my hometown the best-known local character was called "Penny George," but for Dr. Speakman it was a prematurely old gentleman who had a reputation for being converted at every revival.

Each fall the "Governor" would take his stand for Christ and sobriety. But, teased about his new image and uprightness, his resolve would fade, and

long before the cool gusts of the autumn winds would come to send the dead leaves scuttling across the Courthouse lawn, he'd be back in character, and those who seemed to enjoy the spectacle would slip him a quarter and a knowing wink, and might say to their barber later, as he stropped his razor in a cadence that meant to keep time with their wisdom, "You know, that's the trouble with religion. You take old Governor Campbell. There he is stiff as a billy goat again. But if a revival hits town this winter, you know who'll be converted first!"

To discover the need for forgiveness and to have our illusions of self-sufficiency demolished is to pass a milestone on the road to maturity, just as to cry over the death of a loved one gives us complete entry into the human race.

When we fail and find it's necessary to pick ourselves up and try once more, we gain still one more credential that may, eventually, enable us to survive as tempered steel.

Faith doesn't ask us to agree that *everything* that happens is good or furthers the aims of a loving, laboring God. Instead, we now interpret Romans 8:28 to mean that it is *within* tragedy and tears, overcrowded hotels, and crosses on hilltops that God, rather than sending trouble to keep us disciplined into shape, continues to strive with us, for us, beside us, and through us, to take even life's worst tragedies (like the holocaust) and reweave them into garments of celebration.

Many things are *not* as God wills them. They do *not* contribute to God's purpose. But in their wintry centers some potential is often resident, waiting to burst into the springtime blossoms of Providence.

Such is the hallmark of spiritual living.

Persons of faith do not get breaks denied to others. They share in heartaches and heartbreaks with the same impartiality of clouds and rain. They get divorces, fall into bankruptcy, die in accidents, land in intensive care units as often and in the same way as those without any religion at all.

But what they *do* with these happenings—*how* they accept them, *what* they allow them to teach, *what* character they reveal, is the grand and gutsy difference.

There's a Latin motto that reads *ad astra per aspera*: to the stars through difficulty.

So God can use our fears, and brave responses as well.

If we can hold to the belief that God is at least present in whatever happens, then all experience is useful. We need only wait for its ultimate value-moment to come.

And the call to discernment is always to something more profound than simply winning.

In the final paragraphs of John's Gospel, the resurrected Jesus appears to his dispirited friends who, in answer to his question, report that they have fished all night and caught nothing (John 21:1-19). He challenges them to cast their nets on the right side of the boat. This time the nets bulge with a great catch. Only then does he renew his invitation, "Follow me."

He doesn't take them off the bottom or the top. He doesn't say, "See how terrible the fishing is; I'll show you a better use of your time." Instead, he allows them to feel the flush of prosperity, then tests them by a call to something higher than riches.

The word "success" does not appear in the Bible. The word "succession" is there—in the context of laws about inheritance. But not "success," which

*The American Heritage Dictionary of the English
Language* defines as: "The achievement of something
desired, planned, or attempted." And the dictionary
goes on to quote Emily Dickinson: "Success is
counted sweetest / By those who ne'er succeed."

This seems to suggest that success, so long as it is
something out there in front of us, a vision, a hope, is
an essential piece of the human equation. It's what
drives us and tosses us out of bed in the predawn
darkness.

But, if Emily is right, once we are successful,
success may not be all that wonderful.

And successful people are frequently those who
find themselves in the hardest fix of all, like Richard
Cory:

> . . . he was rich—yes, richer than a king—
> And admirably schooled in every grace:
> In fine, we thought that he was everything
> To make us wish that we were in his place.
>
> So on we worked, and waited for the light,
> And went without the meat, and cursed the bread;
> And Richard Cory, one calm summer night,
> Went home and put a bullet through his head.
> (Edwin Arlington Robinson)

Still, the yearnings for recognition and triumph,
for gold medals and gold Krugerrands continue to
make their music in our ears and cause sugarplums
to dance in our heads.

Ford wants to break its sales record and top GM.
The Phillies want to beat the Yankees. And, for

politicians, election night is the Fourth of July and New Year's Eve combined.

I'm a pastor. Do I want to be successful in my leadership? Yes.

We aspire toward success in business, in marriage, in war, in everything we try. Raised arms and scoreboard lights!

But Jesus issues the call *beyond* success—to measure life by one standard that is greater than all the rest: faithfulness.

In his autobiography Martin Luther King, Jr., describes a turning point that occurred one night after he had received another threatening telephone call:

> I got out of bed and began to walk the floor. . . . I was ready to give up. . . . In this state of exhaustion, when my courage had almost gone, I determined to take my problem to God. My head in my hands, I bowed over the kitchen table and prayed aloud. The words I spoke to God that midnight are still vivid in my memory. "I am here taking a stand for what I believe is right. But now I am afraid. The people are looking to me for leadership, and if I stand before them without strength and courage, they too will falter. I am at the end of my powers. I have nothing left. I've come to the point where I can't face it alone."
>
> At that moment I experienced the presence of the Divine as I had never before experienced him. It seemed as though I had never before experienced him. It seemed as though I could hear the quiet assurance of an inner voice, saying, "Stand up for righteousness, stand up for truth. God will be at your side forever." Almost at once my fears began to pass from me.

As a people we enjoy the largest per capita income of any nation in the world, the most freeways, the most television sets, the most bathrooms. But these do not define success for us, except in a very limited way.

True success will always be signaled by other things: moral decency, justice for all, creativity in music and art, sympathy, and an exhilarating sense of what it means to ascend the hills of the unknown and explore the lands of the unlived.

Ralph McGill wrote, following his climbing of Mt. Fuji:

"One stands there, legs trembling, lungs labored, and turns to wait for the sun. The dark awesome slopes of the old mountain are already softening in the flowing light. The eastern sky suddenly blurs crimson. The flaring edge of the sun appears, causing the whole sky to turn rosy; then a deeper vermillion as the round disc of day rises above the horizon. It's a scene worth the climb. Shouts go up. Tired, gleaming faces, streaked with the dark volcanic dust are rapt."

As I finish writing, it is late. The night is dark, the world is still. Dawn, though, will break in a few hours—sweeping across the eastern seaboard, across the plains, across the Rockies to Needles, San Bernardino. Then us. And we will be glad because we will greet that vast tidal wave of energy, believing that we are the children of the day, engaged upon a journey that really matters.

Please
Don't Laugh at Me

Thou shalt be laughed to scorn and had in derision.
(Ezek. 23:32b KJV)

Unless you are a stand-up comedian or a Ringling Brothers clown, you probably don't enjoy being laughed *at*.

A person starved for attention also may deliberately put on an act as a way of being noticed. More often, being laughed at tears away at feelings of self-worth.

The psychological translation of being laughed at runs something like this:

—You've just made a dumb mistake.

—You've mangled the King's English.

—Your pants are torn, your fly is open, or something is falling down.

—You look weird, awkward, out of place.

—What you just said reveals your ignorance of the facts.

—You are drunk.

The fear of ridicule and the psychic pain it brings tends to make us want to avoid providing unintended entertainment for others. So we retreat into silence, unwilling to attempt the sky.

How can we overcome fears of embarrassment—fears that immobilize, paralyze, and chase us into claustrophobic corners of safety? Is the ability to accept being laughed at, without letting such outbursts wound us or terrify us, something learnable? I don't know. I think so, but I'm going to weigh my next sentences. You see, I don't want you to laugh at what I write.

Let's start here: laughter is good.

Homo sapiens is the single creature who laughs, unless braying donkeys or "laughing" hyenas constitute other exceptions.

Laughter is the medicine of the soul, the T-shirt of courage. It rarely injures, but regularly redeems. If we can create some new laughter in the world—even if it costs us in the form of security—it's still a bargain. Even a must if we want to survive.

Ministers make excellent material for gags.

One clergyman is supposed to have memorized the wedding service in order to impress. But, as he stood there the day of the wedding, facing the bride and groom, his mind suddenly went blank.

After some brief seconds of panic he remembered a bit of advice a professor had given him. He was told that if he ever found himself in such a situation of total forgetfulness he should remain calm, then cite familiar verses of Scripture until his composure returned.

Facing the couple, looking out over the roomful of guests, and bracing himself against imminent humiliation, he began: "Father, forgive them; they do not know what they are doing."

The church is sometimes as comical as the Muppets, as down to earth as "All in the Family." One bulletin board announced the following sermon subject for Sunday, "What Is Hell Like?" A few lines below, by way of general publicity, the board said: "You Should Hear Our Choir."

In another congregation, the message was planned around the Old Testament verse: "The fool says in his heart, 'There is no God'" (Ps. 14:1). The outdoor sign that week read:

Dr. Kenneth Brown preaching
11:00 A.M.
What the Fool Said

The church is both a beloved community and a servant community. It also needs, at times, to be the chuckling community where we learn that we can laugh at ourselves and feel good about ourselves at the same time. Few weapons are as successful in calming conflict or disarming opposition.

Sometimes we laugh because we *are* afraid. But laughter may also mean the marching music of resistance. If that were not true, both World Wars I and II would have been lost.

Part of the world's laughter is malicious. More is a spill-over of the human spirit.

If you are the one being laughed at, the fastest relief for psychic pain is not a roll of antacid tablets but joining the fun. Share the moment. You've just achieved an interpersonal rapport no other strategy possibly could. You have met "the enemy" and made him yours.

Another way to handle the discomfort we experience when people laugh at us is to advise ourselves that it's possible to continue to believe in ourselves and what we are doing, even if or when others can't or won't.

You may offer an idea some think is absurd. It may be. But spectator smiles do not make it so. And, if you can withstand those first waves of amusement or ridicule without beating a hasty retreat from your commitment, the second round is almost certain to be one of respectful reconsideration.

Whether it's the Wright Brothers experimenting with flight, or Jimmy Carter announcing in 1974 that he intended to seek the presidency of the United States, there's first a reaction that adds up to incredibility. But persistence often has a good chance of paying off, even if the bandwagon is still far down the road.

We are all kin to Arthur Miller's Willy Loman and to his pathological need to be well liked. We vastly enjoy the sound of applause and reinforcement of peer approval. And, when we must give that up, do without that ego support, we need other intangibles to fall back upon. We need the faith in ourselves that comes out of faith in God.

No one can make us feel inferior without our permission. Yet no one can make us tough enough inside to handle the disapproval of others on any continuing basis except the God within whose will is our peace.

"Only the fear of God," said John Witherspoon, "can deliver us from the fear of man."

And those who stand in the Christ tradition hold that they do not have faith in themselves *because* they find in themselves a goodness or excellence that justifies such a verdict. They believe in themselves because they know God believes in them and accepts them, not for what they have done but for who they are.

It's better to laugh at life and keep our anxiety in reserve for those moments when large issues do hang in the balance.

It was halfway between midnight and dawn when my telephone rang, and a caller, whose voice I didn't recognize, let me know he would be at my house in twenty minutes to discuss a personal problem. I asked him to wait until morning, but agreed that if the need was urgent enough to telephone at 3 A.M., yes, I would talk with him.

I put on my clothes, turned on the outside light, and the lights in the living room, and waited.

He never came.

Two nights later, another call. The same voice, the same message. When I told him I absolutely couldn't see him, he said, "I'm coming anyway. I'll be there within fifteen minutes."

I put on a robe but left the house unlighted and waited for the minutes to pass. Peering out an upstairs window into Mentelle Park below, I could see the lemon-colored puddles the street lights made on the partially snow-covered ground. The bedroom was cold. I sat there shivering.

In spite of a change in our number, enough anonymous calls continued to come over the next several weeks to cause me to jump with a start whenever I heard the ringing of the telephone. Usually it was a friendly call, but the sound still produced flutters of terror. Gradually the calls ceased. The mystery stayed unsolved.

Spring came, and early one morning I found on my desk a note from Cecil, our church custodian. I was asked to call a certain number. Cecil didn't leave notes often. This one must be rather important.

It turned out to be the county jail. The jailer also informed me that, in case I had forgotten it, it was April's Fool's Day.

I went looking for Cecil, not to scold but to congratulate him on his successful trick. When he saw me approaching from the end of a hallway—realizing that, by now, I probably had followed his instruction to call—he doubled up with ecstatic delight. I put my arms around him and laughed at him, laughing at me.

I ran into him several times later that day. Each time his dark face shone, and tears of pleasure ran down his cheeks. It was laughter that brought back my perspective. I lost my fear of the telephone that day—somewhere in that hall pile of sweeping compound, inside the joy of having been Cecil's April Fool.

The only alternative to allowing ourselves to be laughed at may be a cowardly posture that never ventures onto the dance floor, that never forgets the wedding service, but also never drinks from a sparkling cup of self-forgetfulness.

Laughter is more than being April-fooled: it's also a counterbalance to conceit—like a breath of April after a cold January.

We're not attractive.
'Til we've made the plunge into dependency.
Yet we run scared.

> We're afraid of turning forty
> Afraid of being mugged.
> Afraid that life will hurt us,
> Our children come home drugged.
> Of losing our health, of losing our faith.
> The handcuffs, the fence, the chain
> The wall, the rope, the box, the lock—
> The pain of it always being three o'clock
> In the morning.
>   Then
The summer of Christ!
Bark of a tree
Kids inside hula hoops

Sandpipers three, the
Cool silver
Shock
Of plunging into Memorial Day waters.
Our search
Is not to add more years to our life
But more life to our years.

We see the mark of His hand on ours, then
Suddenly our bondage is over. Our fears take
   flight . . .
We're no longer afraid. We're daring and brave
Know there's more
Than our safety to save.

Harvey Cox in his *Feast of Fools* says that "laughter is hope's last weapon. Crowded on all sides with idiocy and ugliness, pushed to concede that the final apocalypse seems to be upon us, we seem nonetheless to nourish laughter as our only remaining defense."

Many of us can recall parents warning us, during our teen years, that in trying to "hang in there" with ideals that seemed right to us we'd better be ready to be laughed at.

We are never entirely prepared to resist such pressures, but such encouragement helps.

And when we hang tough, allowing ourselves to serve as targets, yet not allowing the opinions of others to destroy our own, we begin to see why Thomas More is remembered as *A Man for All*

Seasons, and try to claim a little of that character strain for ourselves. If we can, new qualities of selfhood can start to emerge, solid and sure, like the curvature of violet mountains in the distance as the morning sun lights up the corridors of the day.

Strangers
Could Be Paradise

The Lord is my light and my salvation;
whom shall I fear?
The Lord is the stronghold of my life;
of whom shall I be afraid?

(Ps. 27:1)

Bruce Tennant, a research student at Cal State Dominguez, has compiled an A to Z catalog of fears. Among them are these: *mysophobia*—the fear of dirt; *brontophobia*—the fear of thunder; *kenophobia* —the fear of large, open spaces; *scotophobia*—the fear of darkness; *amenophobia*—the fear of wind; *galenophobia*—the fear of cats; *basiphobia*—the fear of walking. The list concludes with *phobophobia* —the fear of fear, and *panophobia*—the fear of everything.

A neat bundle for everyone.

One fear, though, that pops up regularly in most of our lives is the fear of people we do not know—our fear of strangers.

There are only so many things a mountain can do to us. We can fall off a mountain or get lost trying to climb it. And that's about it.

The sea can make us seasick, maybe drown us. But that's about it.

Human beings, though, are mini-worlds in motion, with power to surprise, love, reject, fool, excite us, or drill a bullet through our chest. They can inform us or inform on us. Sell us merchandise, including stuff we don't need, heal us, scare us, entertain us, smile at us, deceive us, or make us happy. Which will it be from that stranger over there—that tall fellow in the maroon sweater, or the curvaceous blonde with chocolate-bar eyes?

The lottery aspect of such meetings may make us uneasy. Again, they mean additional risks and who needs any more of those?

However, not to risk is worse. It is to adopt strategies of avoidance. It is to stick with those we are sure of, to maneuver ourselves out of reach—the "walking on the other side of the street" syndrome. These tend to shrink our humanity, turn us into stale ponds when we were really created to be clear sparkling streams.

Here are some suggestions, not only for increasing our comfortableness in the presence of strangers, but also for aggressively stepping up our desire to involve ourselves with others:

1. Believe that most people are worth knowing. They are gifts who shouldn't go unclaimed.

2. Tell your mind that the same people who tend

to intimidate you may also be intimidated *by* you. That *that* is in your power to change.

3. Learn the fun of taking the initiative (it *is* learnable). Waiting for the world to come to us isn't as interesting as going out to meet the world. New people to know are as thrilling as new countries to visit.

4. When you approach someone whose identity or name is one you aren't sure of, accept *in advance* the possibility that you may be mistaken and be prepared to smile at your ignorance.

5. Remember that every joined human connection —every end of every strangeness—is another note added to the symphony of peace.

Finding a sliver of glory in another human being can make a day worth living. And calling other people's attention to their own best qualities is a fantastic form of Christian vocation.

Jesse Stuart, Bluegrass poet, wrote one of his most winsome books in the wake of a heart attack which immobilized him for months. He entitled it *The Year of My Rebirth*. It's the story of a man learning to look out on the world with cleansed eyes and gratitude no words seemed able to describe.

As his strength began to return during his months of convalescence Stuart began to take short walks. One came on a Christmas afternoon, through a little grove near his home. The Appalachian air was cold that day, the bark of oaks deep black against the winter landscape. Thickly layered leaves crunched underneath his feet as he sauntered along, drinking in the healing that aloneness often brings.

Suddenly, there stood a stranger—a man with a red beard and open face. He wore a plaid jacket and carried a timber ax. The two men wound up talking briefly together there in the gray afternoon. And that night Jesse Stuart sat down and wrote a few paragraphs about him. He described him as "the man who looked like Christ."

As a minister I'm forever finding new worlds around me, including the discovery of individuals I've been striding past for years without "seeing" or "hearing" them, not perceiving the honest-to-God, one-of-a-kind miracle each one represents.

Then comes a moment of surprising revelation. Suddenly we are praying together in a hospital room or by a grave. We are propped up against one another's bodies around a campfire, or facing a crisis together in which we both have much to gain or lose, and there's a signpost that reads "Emmaus." Like that first Easter, southbound-from-Jerusalem little contingent, we babble our way along, not really knowing one another. We chat about the weather, the Dow Jones, yesterday's scores. Then comes the moment of radical recognition.

In the inn that first Easter Eve with those two disciples, we are told Jesus took bread, blessed, and broke it. Luke says in that moment their eyes were opened and they *recognized* him!

There he is—in that five-year-old's question. In a father's face and a mother's grace, straightening a tie, bandaging a wound. In the apology we made to someone we thoughtlessly offended yesterday. In a walk on a dark night as the moon rises out of a bed of pearl clouds rimmed with platinum.

The table of fellowship around which Christians gather means Jesus comes to them in the midst of the ordinary—meals, work, tears, sleep, sex, politics, salmon-colored tulips, and routine telephone calls. In holiday reunions, in clean shirts, and the public library. In freshly mowed lawns. In a four-year-old letter from one of our kids we stumbled onto in a drawer while looking through old income tax records. In chance meetings that weren't chance at all.

Occasionally a stranger may tell us to mind our own business. We aren't invited in. More often a green light flashes on, and love's traffic starts to flow.

Speculating ominously about what others may be like, even before we have any solid evidence about their attitude or behavior, is known as "projection." We externalize an inward fear. We substitute something about them for our own baseless apprehensions. Our overcoddled ego is struggling to defend itself by attacking an opponent made of straw.

If we leave matters there, projection festers and becomes diseased. Our minds develop infections because we have made them hospitable to lies.

Most fears, whether they have to do with people or phenomena, are based on guesswork.

One study shows that:

40 percent of our fears and worries will never happen.

30 percent are about old decisions we can do nothing about.

12 percent are caused by our misinterpreting the feelings and words of others, assuming they are what they are not.

10 percent are about our personal health which only gets worse as we worry.

Faith delivers us from that sort of false bondage and asks us to pay attention to the hungers of everyone whose life brushes up against our own.

In *Holes in a Stained-Glass Window* Norman Corwin tells how, as a young newspaper reporter in Greenfield, Massachusetts, he was sent to New York to interview 6'4" Heywood Broun, one of the best-known journalists of the time. He had been promised an appointment, but when he dialed from his New York hotel there was no answer. He tried over and over. The phone rang and rang. There was no response. That was Friday. Saturday came. Still no answer. He decided he would have to return emptyhanded, his head full of thoughts about how important this assignment had been to him, yet how incidental it must have been to Broun. But he would make one last try before leaving for the station.

To his amazement Broun answered and invited him over.

For the next two hours they talked and talked. Then, as the young reporter prepared to leave, Broun pulled down a book from the shelf. He thought it had been his best, he said, even if the reading public hadn't thought so. He only had two copies left, but he wanted to give one to Corwin. He inscribed it, encouraging his visitor to press on toward a career on his own. The rainy train ride back to Greenfield was joy incorporated.

On a TV Awards Program, Faye Dunaway spoke about how younger actors and actresses look up to those who have become big successes on stage. The nearest some get to glory is that of the role of understudy. She spoke of these backup roles as "apprenticeships of wonder."

And Carlyle Marney spoke of those who praise and cheer us on as "balcony persons."

Not everyone has a balcony person up there calling bravo, saying our name.

If you do, be glad, clap your hands. Fear can't stand that brand of noise.

Newborn children come into our lives as nameless strangers and steal our hearts away. Strangers brush our lives in chance encounters and turn into dearest friends. On my nineteenth birthday, a stranger picked me up out of a ditch after an accident and held me with the arms of Christ.

Jesus seemed strange—strange to his age, to his family, to conventional ethics, and to those who watched him die that day outside the walls of Jerusalem. But he knocks at our door asking not to be strange any longer.

53

In his presence, and in the recall of his life, strangeness dies. We extend our hand and feel it gripped at the other end.

Dr. Theodore Loder has written:

> Becoming human involves exposing yourself to another, letting someone else see you as you really are, letting them touch you at the core. I am intrigued by some of Michelangelo's statues in which only a portion of the man has been set free from the marble, a torso, a leg, an arm, the hint of a face, and the rest seems to be straining to break out of that stone prison. When I look at those partial figures they stir up in me a deep longing to be completed. An ache to be set free from that which distorts, inhibits and disguises my humanness and wholeness. But, as with those statues, I cannot liberate myself. I need the help of someone else.

One night after a busy day, I hopped into bed early and flipped the television channel to "Wednesday Night at the Movies."

The feature turned out to be "Save the Tiger," a film nominated for an Oscar in the early seventies.

At one point in the story a twenty-two-year-old girl talked with middle-aged Jack Lemmon about those things that appear to give her life significance. One she mentioned was an effort being made to save a certain rare species of animals in danger of becoming extinct.

Of lions and tigers that once roamed the savannahs and wild sections of Africa she said, "I

54

understand they come back to places of remembered beauty."

That phrase haunts me. People, too, need "places of remembered beauty" to return to—not to be caught and trapped in, but as points of reference that enable them to live free from fear and free from hate, free to dream and free to fail.

We may block people out of our lives knowingly and not knowingly. We may look out on the human scene with pinched eyes and padlocked hearts— behave in ways that say to those around us, "There's no room in my life for you," or "Don't come in and look for a place to sit down; I'm fearful of you."

"I'm busy."

Or, "If I let you in, I'll have to give up some of my wrongheaded notions about you. I'm not sure I want to do that."

But when we do allow others into our lives, Jesus often manages to slip in also, quite unnoticed. And that is the beginning of a new world.

A popular song of an earlier time was "Strangers in Paradise." I've come to believe strangers can be paradise, or can at least crack open its front door.

You may contend that paradise is a place—a center of bliss high above earth.

Or you may want to borrow that marvelous line from Mark Twain where Adam said of Eve: "Wheresoever she was, there was Eden."

I'll buy that, but I hope you'll also accept this as

part of the truth about your own life: *today* is Eden, and it's wherever and whenever walls of anxiety come tumbling down, where both strangers and the Stranger described in the Revelation to John (3:20) are welcomed in.

The Right
to Blow Your Stack

There are situations in life in which the absence of
anger would be the essence of evil.
> —Melvin E. Wheatley, Jr.

Those Iowa storms were something, especially in
midsummer, when the humidity would build up
throughout the day and explode into electric zigzags
and bone-rattling thunder around midnight. Light-
ning would slit and snag the sky, turning our Maple
Street living room into a heaving lifeboat.

The storms frightened my mother. Sometimes she
would rouse me from bed to sit with her in the living
room in the darkness until the worst was over, until
nature's fever would break and the delirium subside.

Fortunately, such experiences never made me
afraid of storms. But I've developed my own list of
other fears: an exaggerated need to gain approval, a
fear of wasting time when "wasted time" may be
what my system needs, and the fear of getting
angry—of losing my cool.

Is one of your fears the fear of becoming angry?

Is there something inside you that filibusters so loudly in favor of self-control you find it impossible to allow your own internal volcano to erupt—the hot, backedup lava to go rushing down the hillsides?

Perhaps you know yourself well enough to realize that when that does—wow-ee! The planet begins to shake, your brain starts to smoke, and it takes three days to bring your temperature down. So, you reason, it seems the better part not to let that sort of Three-Mile Island reaction get going.

Most of us fear the thought that we may wind up making idiots of ourselves, say things that can't be taken back. We abhor the thought we may wreck the furniture, make some terrible decisions, or blow a mental gasket.

The alternative to letting anger loose, however, could be worse, because anger doesn't just go away when we tell it to, or disappear when we ignore it. Instead it buries itself in other emotional tissues and we begin inwardly to die.

A person who never gets angry is ill—at least slightly so; for anger is part of a larger emotional spectrum of caring. Bishop Melvin E. Wheatley, Jr., quoted in the headnote, speaks a wise word of reminder to us that there are times when anger is not simply a fallibly human, and normal, response to a situation, but a clear moral duty.

In a delightful essay, Judith Viorst excerpted interviews she had with children on the subject, "What's a good mother like?" At one point she says:

"None of the children expected a mother never to get angry. 'She has to,' said Ted, 'or she'll faint from holding it in.' 'But it's best to remember,' said Randy, 'that when she starts to act real weird, you have to look scared and serious. Don't giggle. When mommies are mad, they get madder when you giggle.'

"'My mommy got so mad,' said Megan, 'she yanked the plate off the table and the mashed potatoes flew in the air.' 'And why,' I asked, pretending I'd never heard such shocking behavior, 'would a mother do a thing like that?' 'Well,' Megan continued, 'she told my brother to eat the potatoes, and Mike said, "Soon." Then she told him to eat the potatoes, and Mike said, "In a minute." And then Mike told her, "How can I eat them? They're cold."'"

Part of the believability of the Bible is that it pictures God on more than one occasion as being utterly furious.

"Who knows the power of your anger?" asked the Psalmist.

Another voice also asks: "Will you be angry with us forever?"

The question we should ask, then, is not, How can I *stop* being angry? But, what forms of anger are good, and what kinds lead me away from God and the self I hope to become?

Think about the last time you were thoroughly "mad." What got you upset? What brought you to the edge of fury, caused your eyes to flash, and your muscular system to go on Red Alert?

Most likely it was something small. Someone was late. Someone made a left turn in front of you without signaling. They lied to you, or about you. You went shopping for groceries and found out everything had gone up again in price. The children stayed out later than they said they would. Your wife forgot. Your husband traded off the car. The neighbors made too much noise.

All of this is part of the package of living, and we can't let it get us down. A five-word apology, a good night's sleep, a little patience, a little love, a little prayer, and we're ready for another day.

Sometimes, though, we know anger that *doesn't* yield to a good night's sleep. Like radioactive waste, it looks as if it may last a lifetime.

We are angry with life itself—or God. Perhaps with ourselves on a deeper, existential level. We don't like being "me," at least not for right now. Or maybe we're angry at our age—the world and the way it's made. Or, looking at other people, we invent adversaries. There's something in us that is hard and won't dissolve.

We smile—yet, underneath a veneer of courtesy we are bitter, afraid, or jealous. Or, we find it impossible to see life as other than, in the end, a junkyard. Beauty and happiness are but mirages. Underneath life's piles of transitory possessions and impermanent achievements there is nothing but loneliness and ice.

John Wesley, following his conversion, spoke about being "strangely warmed" within. Maybe inner warmth represents a greater need than air-conditioned department stores.

Perhaps what we need to do is say: "God, I am angry, but I don't want that anger to be destructive. Life's too short! And there's too much wonder in the world to allow it to become lost in a thick blanket of smog. God, draw me closer to yourself. Let your Spirit play on my spirit in ways that will enable me to convert this injury into some kind of personal asset. And please help me say no to self-pity. That's anger, too—anger at myself for being who I am, at you for making me the way I am."

Anger riveted merely to pride or convenience has one outstanding by-product: stress. A more productive kind of anger would be aimed at a world where, with so many resources and so much knowledge, there still remain tens of millions of people who are dirt poor, hundreds of millions who can't read, legions with no faith or dream at all.

Some anger simply screams out for ventilation. We feel better and function better, once we've flung the mashed potatoes into the air.

Others dump tea into the Boston Harbor and get a republic started. Produce a new walk-light at a busy intersection where children cross, or arouse people to do something about neighborhood crime. There's prophetic anger that won't let things stay the way they are.

Said Coach Paul Westhead of his star player, "Magic Johnson," after his Lakers basketball team had won the NBA Championship in 1980, "He realizes the need we have and flows to that need."

Injustice to ourselves is no problem. We rail against it. We fight to correct it. We cry out in indignation. We make demands for reparations. We've been mistreated. We did not get what was our due. We were overcharged. We suffered unfairly. We have our rights! We will not be dumped on! We will go to court! We will cause so much trouble for our oppressor he'll be sorry he ever did this to us!

But when injustice is the lot of *another*, when someone else has no job, or enough to eat, or a place to live, or is discriminated against, is victimized by hate or dies a premature death because of ignorance or untreated disease, that becomes easier for us to live with. I have a feeling, though, that prayers of gratitude for our own abundance can begin to sound slightly suspect in the courts of the Lord, become self-congratulatory rather than the mark of the saint.

Such an attitude is the largest flaw in what is sometimes spoken of as the "religious right"—those whose main concern appears to be the right of the already secure to pray in the public schools, to arrest pornographers, or to cut taxes—who denounce welfarism, yet never cry out—ever—from another bleeding side, that of the body of man.

"Magic Johnson realizes our need and flows to it."

Do we? Whatever we do, or say, or feel that communicates to another that his or her life has both beauty and importance is part of that flow, part of the river of love.

We don't need upbraiding today as much as we need bright and good goals to live for. We need to be people caught up in the grandeur of things, in the excitement of working in the beauty of creating, and in the satisfaction of serving. Boredom and cynicism are the real enemies of the true life, not violations of rules.

We have theological trouble with a perfect Jesus, angrily upsetting the tables of the money-chargers in the temple. Yet something inside us lets out a cheer—"Let 'em have it, Lord"—and anger becomes, not a violation of divinity, but a proof of a total humanity.

If we can be outraged at congressional corruption, angel-dust peddlers, rent gouging, old people eating dog food to survive, and recommended legal devices to avoid laws established to produce an integrated society, then this may add up to some glimmer of evidence that we are made in the image of a God who became angry enough at sin to do something about it.

The price, though, was high.

Do you remember heady optimisms of the Kennedy years? The world seemed so young then. We all felt idealistic. We were convinced we stood on some incontrovertible threshold of greatness, on the doorstep of a shining, open future.

Then, assassination.

War.

Shortages.

Suddenly, we were wretched, old, and diseased,

and seemed to enter a pessimistic freeze of the spirit, the terminal death pronouncement of hope.

Those are, of course, extremes—distant ends of the human scale.

And, in the middle, life continues. Gold trombones still play, which is the presupposition of this book. And a better world continues to be hammered out on anvils of sacrifice, God helping, if we are determined to replace a reign of despair with a song of celebration, sung by pilgrims enroute to a City.

It's Only Money—
Oh Yeah?

Fraidy cat, fraidy cat, sitting on the fence.
Tryin' to make a dollar out of fifteen cents.
　　　　　　　　—Childhood taunt

Many of our fears have to do with money, and I
don't know anyone who doesn't spend a good deal of
energy fretting over the stuff. Those who have too
much worry about someone stealing it. Those with
too little worry about starving. A woman recluse in
Indianapolis died, and a garbage can containing two
million dollars *in cash* was found in her bedroom!
One person loses thousands in an evening at Las
Vegas; another barely makes it on a subsistence
pension.

Young people in the sixties looked at our society
and concluded there wasn't much of anything else
the gray flannel crowd *did* think about, so they
tickled our noses with tulips. The seventies arrived,
bringing a new weather system of conservatism, the
decay of détente, and the Bakke case.

Now it's the eighties, and up there with the red telephone and nuclear button as a threat to everyone's future is another source of fear: how to cope with inflation.

Older persons, their life expectancies expanded, wonder if life or money will be exhausted first. Rents of $500 to $1,000 a month are common. Gasoline has quadrupled in price, and the word "trillion" is now part of our vocabulary in discussing national finances.

In his book, *Prayers*, Michel Quoist has a poignant meditation entitled "Prayer Before a Twenty-Dollar Bill." In it he finds himself thinking about all the different things that little green paper rectangle is capable of accomplishing, and what it may have already accomplished as it has passed from hand to hand to hand.

It's able to buy health care for someone who desperately needs it.

Or send a young person to college.

It can feed and bless, shelter and make whole, buy trumpets and travel.

Or it can prompt someone to rob, to make war. To wreck a world.

No wonder money frightens us. Bills, bank statements, price tags, credit cards, pocketbooks, interest rates, bus fares, Wall Street, allowances for a ten-year-old.

Failure to possess it can slam a door. Possessing it, rather than laying problems to rest, can wind up rearranging them. How to deal responsibly with one's resources, especially in the light of the disparities between a Beverly Hills and Bangladesh, is as demanding a test of discipleship as there is.

Someone has said, "Money is not the only thing in life, but it is surely way ahead of whatever is in second place." Which is another obscenity, unless we take such a remark to mean that money can achieve and enhance the will and purposes of God if it is managed and invested by reverent and grateful human beings.

In the family of my youth, my mother was the bill payer. We had no checking account in those days. But, on the first two or three days of the month, she would make the Main Street rounds discharging our obligations.

First she would write out a list of the bills on the back of a used modest envelope:

rent, or mortgage	$32.00
light bill	1.05
food	35.00
church envelope	4.00
telephone	2.75
insurance	1.50
shoes	3.95

So it went. And thanks to her judgment and prudent management, we kept in the black. Narrowly at times, but almost always in the black.

Today, the cost of survival is higher. Now a jar of peanut butter is $2.50, a pair of shoes $60. Keeping the wolf from the door is almost more than most people can manage.

We have other demands, too, that put us under stress. We "owe" things to one another in our families—mostly time and attention.

We hear the church say, "Now we'd like everyone to do this."

At home, a dandelioned or oxalis-plagued yard begs for care; the house cries out for fixing. Our employer wants better performance. Schools need our involvement. The "Y" is trying to build a new swimming pool.

We open the mail. More bids for energy and money. Social life—more claims.

We open the Bible to find relief from incessant importuning only to find: "Discharge your obligations . . . pay tax and toll" (Rom. 13:7 NEB). We wonder how we can ever get caught up, paid up. Perhaps we should go ahead and simply pronounce ourselves bankrupt.

Faith, though, is made for such dilemmas, and the church, at its best, has always been a workshop in priorities.

It is there to remind us that God never asks us for what we do not have. God wants to deliver us from the cowardice that is made later to confess: "I was afraid, and I went and hid your talent in the ground" (Matt. 25:25).

Fear can be allayed if we will sort out priorities— "Thou shalt have no other gods before me"—in order to make decent and responsible choices, and then let the balance go.

The use of money and time aren't all that different.

You who are beyond time, Lord, you smile to see us
    fighting it.
And you know what you are doing.
You make no mistakes in your distribution of time to
    men.
You give each one time to do what you want him to
    do.
But we must not lose time
   waste time,
   kill time,
For time is a gift that you give us,
But a perishable gift,
A gift that does not keep.

Lord, I have time,
I have plenty of time,
All the time that you give me,
The years of my life,
The days of my years,
The hours of my days,
They are all mine.
Mine to fill, quietly, calmly,
But to fill completely, up to the brim,
To offer them to you, that of their insipid water
   You may make a rich wine such as you made once
   in Cana of Galilee.
I am not asking you . . . , Lord, for time to do this and
    then that,
But your grace to do conscientiously, in the time that
    you give me,
   what you want me to do.

Paul says, "Leave no claim outstanding against
you, except that of mutual love" (Rom. 13:8 NEB).

Even if we should find it possible to settle most of
our obligations, we can't pay them all. Nor should
we want to. It is no achievement to be entirely free of
debt, or trumpet such nonsense as "I have paid my
way," "I have kept your commandments," or "I
don't owe anybody anything."

What child could repay his parents?

Life is no quid pro quo. It is needing one another.
It isn't being "paid up"; it's living with a permanent
"accounts payable."

Betty Ford is reported to have said of marriage:
"Successful marriages are not based on 50-50. It's
more like 70-30, with each side giving 70."

We begin with nothing. We've no possessions at
all. Then, beginning with a first fluffy stack of
diapers, our accumulation career begins. If we are
fortunate enough to be born into a family that can
provide, the list grows rapidly. Soon we have several
outfits of clothes. Then toys, bicycles, a wrist watch
for a birthday. A savings account. We grow some
more, start earning income of our own. The list
grows longer. Soon we're into furniture, wheels,
houses, jewelry, things to wear. If we enter business
we try to increase those holdings and resources. We
buy stocks and bonds. If we're farmers we need
machinery. If we're lawyers, we need a library. More
closets. Rooms. Equipment for living. Experiences
of having.

Somewhere along the trip, though, we cross some
invisible equator and start to unload. Now we need
smaller living space, fewer gadgets, less luggage, less

to make us "happy." And, as we enter the home stretch, not much at all. The things we are attached to now are our friends, our faith, a sense of being alive to the world and what God is trying to do with the world. To be on good terms with ourselves, to have love in our lives, hope, a sense of being needed, a way to contribute, eyes to take in beauty—these things that aren't things at all but matters of the heart are the important realities. Realities that define us in terms of our character and our capacity to love and forgive. Now we are what we cherish—not what we own.

Two-thirds of Jesus' parables are about money. His stories do not reflect a negative attitude about wealth. Instead, they emphasize the importance of the ways people use it and to what purposes: to show neighbor love, or to squander it in vanity.

Here are a few of those unforgettable parables:
The rich man and his barns—Luke 12:15-21.
Caesar's inscription on money—Mark 12:14-17.
The widow's gift of a penny—Mark 12:41-44.
Treasures that do not rust or cannot be stolen—
    Matthew 6:19-21.
Choice between God and mammon—Luke 16:13.
The lost coin—Luke 15:8-10.
Paying for the case of a wounded man—Luke
    10:35.

In other places in the Bible, too, we are cautioned about money's power to destroy as well as to serve. Peter said to [Simon of Samaria, a sorcerer], "Your silver perish with you, because you thought you could obtain the gift of God with money!" (Acts 8:20).

"For the love of money is the root of all evils; it is through this craving that some have wandered away from the faith and pierced their hearts with many pangs" (I Tim. 6:10).

"The genuineness of your faith, [is] more precious than gold" (I Pet. 1:7).

There are dozens of other sayings about money.

Toots Shor once observed, "Money is for throwing off the back of trains."

My dad would say, "You can lie down beside a bushel basket of it and starve to death."

It couldn't buy happiness for Howard Hughes, or J. Paul Getty.

At the same time, life is hard if, lacking it, you cannot feed your family, buy shoes for your children, pay your creditors, or if you get up each morning worrying about how to make it through to a next payday.

It's easy to scoff at the irrelevance of money if we have a plentiful supply. If we don't, concern about it will blot out the sun.

People kill for money. They lie, prostitute their own flesh, sell their souls. On an oversold flight, an airline representative boarded the already filled plane, bound for Dallas, and offered anyone present a bonus of $250, plus a ticket on a subsequent flight for surrendering a seat. A half-dozen passengers quickly accepted. The proverbial political wisdom is "everyone has his price," but I remember someone who said no to that.

Money is stored-up power. It's a golden key that

turns inside a golden lock to liberate and fulfill. Or it can cut and curse, poisoning the water.

I once received a call from a legal aid society, and a police officer's voice on the other end described a nineteen-year-old girl whose home was in Chicago, but who had come to Los Angeles to visit friends. She was killed while riding as a passenger in an automobile. She was from a poor, black family, and the problem was how to get her body back to her mother. I called a church member to see if our deacons might help.

I had called the right number. Gloria got in her car, went to the mortuary, and wrote her own check for $450 in order that the girl's body could be returned.

Money can do holy things, but it can't buy a conscience at rest.

It can buy open-heart surgery or a dialysis machine. But it cannot buy respect. It can buy toys, but not Christmas. It can buy sex, but not love.

It can't buy life. If it could, I would resign my job and go into the fund-raising business with the thought of buying back the life of my twenty-one-year-old daughter, killed in a car accident on Easter Sunday in 1970.

Each December I sort through a "save" pile until I find some favorite lines which first appeared in *McCall's* magazine. Though they speak of the rightful inheritances of children, they address everyone:

In the long twilight of the
year, the faces of the children grow luminous.

Rosy with cold, arabesqued
with snowflakes, leaning into the wind, or drowsing
before the fire, their eyes large, they
look and listen, as if they glimpsed the peripheries of
miracle
or heard a soundless music in the air. From the innocent
kingdom of implicit belief to that uncomfortable
arena where the implacable mind battles the
intractable heart, the
faces of children at Christmas are lighted
with visions of things to come.

What shall we give the children?
It seems certain that they will travel roads
we never thought of, navigate strange seas, cross
unimagined boundaries, and glimpse horizons beyond
our power to visualize. What can we give them to take
along? For the wild shores of Beyond, no toy or
bauble will do. It must be something more, constructed
of stouter fabric discovered among the
cluttered aisles and tinseled bargain counters
of experience,
winnowed from what little we have
learned. It must be devised out of responsibility
and profound caring—a homemade
present of selfless love. Everything changes but the
landscape of the heart.

What shall we give the children?
Attention, for one day it will be too late.
A sense of value, the inalienable place of the individual
in the scheme of things, with all
that accrues to the individual—self-reliance,
courage, conviction, self-respect, and respect for others.
A sense of humor. Laughter leavens life,

74

The meaning of discipline. If we falter at discipline,
life will do it for us.
The will to work. Satisfying work is the lasting joy.
The talent for sharing, for it is not so much
what we give as what we share.
The love of justice. Justice is the bulwark against violence
and oppression and the repository
of human dignity.
The passion for truth, founded on precept and example.
Truth is the beginning of every good thing.
The power of faith, engendered in mutual trust. Life
without faith is a dismal dead-end street.
The beacon of hope, which lights all darkness.
The knowledge of being loved beyond demand or
reciprocity, praise, or blame, for these so
loved are never lost.

What shall we give the children?
The open sky, the brown earth, the leafy tree, the golden
sand, the blue water, the stars in their courses,
and the awareness of these. Birdsong, butterflies, clouds,
and
rainbows. Sunlight, moonlight, firelight.
A large hand reaching down for a small hand, impromptu
praise, an unexpected kiss, a straight answer.
The glisten of enthusiasm and a sense of wonder. Long
days
to be merry in and nights without fear.
The memory of a good home.

A magazine ad for a telephone company shows a
network of thousands of tiny different-colored
wires, then suggests typical messages that may be

hurtling back and forth through all that intricate copper weave:

"I love you." "I need money." "I'm coming home!" "How is Bob?" "I'm in some big trouble." "The operation was a success and Judy is O.K." "Can you believe it—they hired me!"

This same copper interchange carried millions of stories about conflict, contracts, and congratulation. And we have to find a way to live with it all—to celebrate simple moments made out of glimpsed birds in V-flight above our morning coffee. Money is never valuable for itself—the best it can do is point.

A woman who suffered through a long debilitating illness left a suicide note which read "Good-bye rotten world." We sympathize with such despair, and do not judge, do not blame.

But standing against that judgment is some graffiti I saw crudely stenciled on a wall along a Laguna Beach front. It read: "Go ride the music!"

That's our summons. Climb aboard.

Accepting Yesterdays

The beginning of mercy is to be merciful to one's self.
—Anonymous

Somewhere Søren Kierkegaard has written that anxiety is the "next day." And, yes, it is the future that scares us, from peace to pieces.

But yesterday also has a formidable power over us.

As memory, the past can delight and make us mellow. Its flip side, though, is torment if what we most easily remember are our mistakes, things we would leap to change if we could, but can't.

Looking ahead, the Christian message is statable in one word: *hope*. Looking back, our best single-word definition is *forgiveness*.

The Good News of Jesus is: "Go your way; your faith has made you well" (Mark 10:52), which seems to include past, present, and future.

The fires of sunset fill up the western
  sky again,

Ready to receive within their orange heat
All that deserves forgetting:

> Those neat, slick plans that fell apart,
> The things we never got around to start,
> The fears, the fuss, the unsung songs,
> Whatever that could be labeled wrongs
In love's incinerator now belong.

The beginning of mercy is to be merciful
   to oneself
So we are told. Now night's horizon's edged in gold

> And sleep will bring us holy rest,
> Forgiveness add us to the blest,
> Dreams will set us free once more,
> Then a pink knock upon the door
As God calls home the stars.

A golf pro at nearby Marshall Canyon Country Club has a vanity license plate that reads "Ex-con." He's determined not to let a prison background forever cripple his life. That tag is his own obvious badge of courage.

With the past thus drained of its power to make us miserable, we're in position for a next step: to fall in love with what is going on in our life—*now*.

There are many, many ways to bring that about. We can fall in love with people, our work, roses, history, literature, cities, law, science, architecture, teaching, theology, the sea, athletics, children, politics, art, medicine, business, and butterflies. Everyone and everything is eligible—except money.

Life remains the only wealth. To possess it and

celebrate it, to be caught up in the passion for meaning, to love is to inherit the earth.

Since I was in the fifth grade I have wanted to be a writer. I was the editor of a high school paper, *The Needle,* and a college yearbook, *The Zenith.* I love the wild, elegant things you can do with words when you string them together like colored, odd-shaped laundry, and hang them on clotheslines of imagination.

Then, there came a day when, at age forty-nine, I received a telegram telling me that a manuscript I had submitted had been selected for a national prize and that it would be published.

A ton of feeling surged over me that day. I thought of all those years—my mother and father, my wife and children, my high school English teacher—but the only prayer I could manage was "Thank you. Thank you." It seemed enough.

Yet the present is all we possess. The past is part of us when we speak, laugh, love, cry, or say "I." And the future tints our dreams, making promises even before it arrives. But *now* is the only time that's unmistakably our own.

James Thurber said we should not look forward in fear, or backward in regret, but around us in awareness.

That sounds like great advice.

But how can we pull it off? How can we get into the energy-saving business when it comes to ridding ourselves, both of worry over what lies in front of us and remorse over what lies behind us—emotional fires that smoulder and burn, causing us to lose sight of the jewel that is the moment closest at hand?

We begin to experience hints of liberation when we decide to make peace with yesterday.

Rabbi Robert Kahn of Houston pointed this out. He said: "Don't let yesterday destroy today. You have failures in the past. You have failed in business, failed a course, failed a friend, failed your family. But who has not? No one is perfect, no one is successful. Don't dwell on those failures. Make peace with yesterday."

After reading that I found my own way to say it:

> You can't unring a bell,
> You can't unshine a star,
> You can't retrieve a word you've said,
> The things that are just are.
>
> But you can accept the truth,
> You can breathe deep and free,
> You can, out of emptiness, create
> A fact, and a flame, called Me.

We have to learn to let go—realize that not to forgive ourselves is not to accept what God stands ready to provide.

And the choice isn't that complicated. We can either go with the light, or stay crouched in the dark—burdened and afraid. We can sing or disgorge obscenities. Trust the offer of freedom, or dismiss the Christian gospel as primitive nonsense.

So we choose Christmas and faith. Easter and hope. We choose Love, and we choose one another.

We also have a need to loosen our hold on a tomorrow that, more than likely, will turn out differently from what we expected or planned.

An enjoyable responsibility of ministers is talking with couples who plan to be married. But one of the things they worry about, in addition to wondering if they are really helping prospective brides and grooms face up to the implication of their decisions, is the possibility of allowing the time and place of the ceremony to be forgotten.

One autumn I met with a couple who told me they wanted to be married in the home of a relative on New Year's Day. I counseled with them over a period of weeks. Then, as the date drew closer, I drove by the designated location on a December afternoon to make sure I could locate it easily. I didn't want to wind up wandering around on a strange street, looking for the correct house a few minutes before the processional was set to begin.

I also alerted my wife to the New Year's Day appointment, asking her to remind me so that, in the midst of an exciting football game or other holiday distraction, I wouldn't ignore where I was supposed to be.

I felt sure I might forget it. New Year's weddings aren't that common.

You're probably thinking: after all that, you *still* forgot!

No.

I remembered.

I wasn't even late.

But, as I drove up in front of the house that day, about four o'clock in the afternoon, I was surprised that no cars were parked in the vicinity of the house where the wedding was scheduled to take place. And even more surprised when a lady answered the door and told me the couple had quarreled at the last moment. They had canceled the ceremony without letting me know.

Yes, anxiety is the next day.

Another time I was asked to conduct a funeral service an elderly woman had carefully pre-arranged. But she outlived her family and all her friends. Not one person showed up on the day of the service. Only the director and myself were there to stand beside her casket—to pray and remember how special each human life is.

But anxiety can also be, and will be yesterday unless it is conquered and brought into a perspective of acceptance and peace. Remembering things we have done in the past that were selfish or evil can be instructive, can save us from repeating them. Most errors, however, simply need to be allowed to die so that the journey can go on. To give up the right to extricate ourselves from all that has been can be both masochistic and conceit masquerading as remorse.

A young woman in Newport Beach took her own life recently, and this is how a beach-front reporter told her story:

There were sedatives and sleeping pills still left, police said, when they found Rosemary Russell

Tuesday morning, along with a "to-whom-it-may-concern" note.

If her careful instructions are followed, the golden life she had built for herself will be dismantled. The house she lived in, in Dover Shores, the dog she owned, the Mercedes she drove will belong to others.

But she wants to serve as an example, she said in one letter to a pair of friends. "Just do me a favor," she wrote, "so it won't be for nothing. Don't let the pursuit of money and success interfere in the beautiful relationship you two have. As long as you have each other, and a strong faith in God, you'll want for nothing else."

As long as you have each other and faith in God, you can make it. But without faith, and without community, the will to live flounders and finally falls.

The ability to enjoy each moment, being on speaking terms with ourselves, and good eye-contact with the person who sits opposite us at table. Are these the main prizes of our existence? At least some of them are close. And to trade any one for a room at the top would be a bad deal.

But Rosemary Russell, in her note, also mentioned another of the silver hinges on which happiness swings: belief in God, that Reliance that turns us into giants, that can be to us something more valuable than anything else the world has on display.

Sometimes I'm asked: "How do you get faith? Where did you get your faith? What do you do if you *want* to believe and can't."

It sounds like that's where Rosemary wanted to be, but didn't know how to get there. Or perhaps faith without love isn't enough. These are the twin treasures you know are worth all the rest, but you must be honest, and belief is hard—especially in light of a world that often seems in danger of pulling apart at the seams, God or no God.

I won't be silly and say there's a plain answer. Neither will I protest that there isn't any answer. There is!

Faith is journey, not a set of fixed, bloodless ideas.

It's an act of the heart that opens a door to invite God in. But it is not a bundle of certainties, or paid-up insurance, or insulation from harm.

Rather it's an order of surrender, a yes! coupled with the willingness to walk with others who also are attempting to say yes with their lives. It is to believe that Jesus, rather than being a distant figure out of the historical long-ago, is the Lord of all time, including the next five minutes.

Faith is finding God in our yesterdays. Hope is confidence both in our tomorrows and in whatever future is on its way.

And gratitude is a seed, planted in the brown and waiting earth, which after winter's hard work and a springtime shout of resurrection produces borders of orange-gold nasturtiums.

What If Something Should Happen to _____?

If I flew to the point of sunrise,
or westward across the sea,
your hand would still be guiding me,
your right hand holding me.
                    (Ps. 139:9-10 JB)

Today we stood in church to sing:

Give to the winds thy fears;
    Hope and be undismayed;
God hears thy sighs and counts thy tears,
    God shall lift up thy head.
                    (Paul Gerhardt, 1656)

And those words seemed to carry with them a lift for all the people I felt standing around me.

"Give to the winds thy fears . . ."

Some fears, we've been saying, have creative value for us. Some even wind up saving our lives. Others drive us into each other's arms to be loved and comforted. Still others are responsible for bringing into play reserves of bravery we never knew we had. But there are fears that need to be confronted and exorcised from our inner world as masked robbers or faceless ghosts.

One is the nagging thought that something terrible is about to happen to someone whose life and safety is of crowning concern to us.

A woman drops her husband off at O'Hare Airport, on the edge of metropolitan Chicago. They kiss good-bye. He hurries into the terminal, folded newspaper under his arm, and in a jiffy he's flying off into the dawning day at 35,000 feet.

Driving home, little whitecaps of worry course through her 7:20 A.M. thoughts: What if something should happen to Jack? What would happen to all of us?

A hypothetical headline dances across the journal of her unconscious: "Flight 44 Missing. All Aboard Presumed Lost."

Nineteen-year-old Joe goes off to spend three months in Europe. He'll telephone home every two weeks to assure his dad and mother he's okay. He'll meet all sorts of interesting people, use his Eurail pass, ski in the Alps. He's a smart kid—not prone to do reckless things. Yet, there are so many problems he could encounter. And he's so far away . . .

"Do you suppose we're right in letting him go?" says his mother to her husband in a bit of pillow talk the night before his leaving.

In a world filled with daring, first-time-walks-to-kindergarten, dirt bikes, off-to-college-departures, marriages, accidents, crimes, and heart attacks—a world where such contingencies are matched by an even longer list of magnificent ways our lives become entangled with one another—that we should worry about something happening to those who are precious is as expectable as tulips in April.

"What if . . . ?"

It would take a computer bigger than the pyramids to produce print-outs of the hazards every life-filled hour contains.

In pondering a response to mass uncertainty it is useful to distinguish between a normal preparation for an unlived tomorrow and the peace-wrecking anxieties that wind up protecting no one at all.

Somewhere, somehow, we must find a way to accept the truth that we are not God and must not allow ourselves to take that kind of responsibility upon our shoulders, as if it were either proper or within our power.

If this were not reason enough to loosen our grasp, and surrender to God's protection those we would spare from hurt, let it be said here that to assume such an omnipresent, sheltering role, even if it were possible, would be a violation of the freedom of the one we care about. While parading as love, it would not be love at all. The love we learn from the Christ is not possessive. It is not validated by believing that if *we* are not guiding and protecting, no one else could be. Otherwise, love that begins nobly will wind up as nail-biting self-idolatry.

So we wrong others if we attempt to control them by our fears. Sometimes God's call to us is not to serve or die, but to *relax.*

Better is the spirit of the old prayer which prays:

Make us strong to commit those we love to Thy never-failing care. In our perplexity may we trust where we cannot understand, knowing that the eternal God is our refuge and underneath are the everlasting arms.

If the gospel means anything genuinely decisive for us, it means we must give up our private claims of sovereignty and let God be God.

We must learn to let life unfold on its own terms, allow the past to depart unregretted, the future arrive unresented. Let go and let God.

Dr. Donald Shelby, a United Methodist pastor in Santa Monica, California, who is always saying things better than almost anyone else I know, once said in a Children's Day sermon:

"Our birth is not ended with the first gasp of breath and the first cry of our lungs. We are born for innumerable births and rebirths. We are forever pushing our way into new worlds. Through countless experiences, by high ecstasies and deep sorrows, we explore heights and depths inside ourselves. Our bodies grow and their capacity and skills increase. Awareness grows as one experience after another pours through our senses into memory, as feelings and emotions respond. Our minds grow and creative thought and intuition and imagination are enlarged. Above all, and including all, our spirit grows—that essence which manifests who we really are."

To grow is to outgrow. It is to leave the nest, and watch others leave, with our blessing. It is to know that we will hurt awhile. It is to acknowledge the impermanence of jobs, families, friendships, political entities, ideas. It is to accept the truth that, while there's much that is fragile and fleeting, life's one superb banquet just the same.

Here are some biblical sources that might help achieve peace of heart when you commit the life of someone you care about into those hands that are stronger and more loving than your own.

When someone is leaving on a trip:

> Psalm 139
> Isaiah 43:1-5
> Romans 8:38-39

When a loved one suffers pain or may die:

> Matthew 14:28-36
> I Peter 4:12-19
> Hebrews 12:1-11

When someone is in trouble: financial or legal, or is caught up in a scandal:

> Psalm 46
> Luke 12:22-31
> II Corinthians 4:7-18

When a marriage is in danger:

Ephesians 4–5

I John 4:7-21

I Corinthians 13

When someone is depressed or weighed down with grief:

II Corinthians 5:3-4

Romans 5:1-5

II Timothy 1:7

When there is misunderstanding and estrangement:

Psalm 27

Matthew 5:21-24

Matthew 5:43-48

A constructive approach to fear means to take seriously the Bible's insistence that God is interested in us and cherishes each possibility our humanity contains. It means cultivating the art of liking ourselves, laughing at ourselves, trusting ourselves, accepting the notion that we are among the beautiful people.

We can also outwit our opposition by turning our interest, attention, and affection outward—finding regular occasions to praise others, to listen, to care, and to enjoy—to learn that behind most of the walls that scare us are not ghosts but human uniqueness, yearning to find its way out of jail.

And we can come to believe there are powerful spiritual resources at our disposal, which is the nagging conviction that seemed to keep asking me to create this book.

In his *Experiment in Depth* (Routledge & Kegan

Paul, Ltd., 1976), P. W. Martin tells about some terrifying experiences of his own as a soldier in the trenches during World War I and the discovery of a "something more" quality that sustained him in the midst of shrieking shells and the thought that any moment could be his last. In the midst of this noisy hell he suddenly located within himself an isle of calm. "Whereas a moment before I had been shaking with fear, it became as if I had down the center of my body a cylinder of steel."

The Sunday after John F. Kennedy was killed I faced one of the largest congregations I had ever seen in my ministry. I had written a sermon in midweek, and, since it was the Sunday before Thanksgiving Day, I based it on something Paul had written to a group of Christians at Thessalonica. "In *everything* give thanks." Then came Friday. The bullets, the blinding national pain.

I said some different things that Sunday than I had planned, but the text stayed the same. Even out of crucifixions, new mutations arise. Sometimes the right spelling of the gospel seems to be serendipity.

It was once said of Marlon Brando, "He acts as if he had an angel inside of him, and sometimes it's as if it were more than he could contain."

There are angels inside all of us. Some are asleep; others are dead, or need to be revived. And sometimes they are more than we can contain. We might *never* meet them if life were clearly predictable, and the fate of those we love immune from harm.

Part of the work of God's Spirit is to wake up our

angels. It is to help us believe that even our most demanding hours help make us whole.

An Irish benediction may help us say at least some of what is in our hearts to those whom we would touch with traveling mercies:

> May the blessing of light be on you, light without and
>   light within.
> May the blessed sunlight shine on you, and warm
>   your heart
>   till it glows like a great peat fire, so that the stranger
>   may come
>   and warm himself at it, and also a friend.
> And may the light shine out of the two eyes of you,
>   like a candle set in two windows of a house
>   bidding the wanderer to come in out of the storm.
> And may the blessing of rain be on you, the soft sweet
>   rain.
> May it fall upon your spirit, so that all the little
>   flowers
>   may spring up, and shed their fragrance on the air.
> And may the blessing of the great rains be on you,
>   may they beat upon your spirit and wash it fair and
>   clean,
>   and leave there many a shining pool, where the
>   blue of heaven
>   shines reflected, and sometimes a star.
> And may the blessing of the earth be on you, the great
>   round earth.
> May you ever have a kind greeting for them you pass
>   as you go along the road.
> May the earth be soft under you, when you rest upon it
>   tired at the end of a day.

And may it rest easy over you at the last when you lay
    out under it,
May it rest so lightly over you that your spirit may be
    off
  from under it quickly—up and off and on its way to
  God.

ONE DAY AT A TIME

"Fear not, for I have redeemed you;
I have called you by name, you are mine."
(Isa. 43:1)

Is there a man of you who by anxious
thought can add a foot to his height?
(Matt. 6:27 NEB)

In the previous chapter we talked about the fear of something happening to persons we care about—our children, parents, wives, husbands, or friends. We worry about their safety, their happiness. We know we can't control the destiny of others, but our hearts have trouble buying that.

From there, let's go on to review a few of the anxieties which have to do with ourselves—the fear we may lose a job, get cancer, be injured, or die.

That such catastrophes loom up out of nowhere to strike innocent people down, that there are things in the world such as mental illness and leukemia, that couples find it necessary to divorce, that kidnappings take place, that earthquakes, hurricanes, fires, and floods are part of the makeup of history can't be denied if one takes even an occasional look at a daily newspaper.

Such information, in massive doses, will be depressing and intimidating if we do not also take the time to balance that picture with other time spent walking in gardens, going to concert halls, playing softball, worshiping God, reading history, and celebrating birthdays.

There's a tradition that comes from Mexico. Friends gather to sing outside your bedroom window early on the morning of your birthday. How could anyone lose faith in either life or love after a gift like that?

But let's be serious. How can we know as much as we do about the dangers of life and still sing and sleep, paint and dance our way through our borrowed years?

The question is too grand and far-reaching to be answered in a book, but we see *people* answering it by triumph over difficulties, by laughter and prayer, by the wonder of love and the authority of trust.

Norman Cousins speaks of older adults who continue to participate enthusiastically in art and politics, despite arthritis and maybe a visit to the coronary care unit, as persons who have a challenging appointment with life rather than a certain date with death.

Jesus apparently had that in mind when, in the Sermon on the Mount, he challenged us not to be anxious about food or clothing, or the future, but to "consider the lilies of the field" (Matt. 6:28) and enjoy each moment for itself before it becomes a memory.

The commandment to love also is instructive. John interprets:

> There is no fear in love, but perfect love casts out fear.
> For fear has to do with punishment, and he who fears
> is not perfected in love. (I John 4:18)

Another skill worth study is set forth in Stanley Keleman's *Living Your Dying* (Random House, 1976). Mr. Keleman argues that, while we do not know much about death, we know a lot about dying and get a great deal of practice at it almost from the time we are born.

A friend of mine has a 1948 Lincoln, a car he has learned to adore. He tells me he is under pressure to get rid of it because now it costs so much to run. One of these days, he realizes, he must say good-bye to a dear friend.

We are constantly saying good-bye, letting go of a string of yesterdays, of childhood and children, friends, familiar houses, jobs, 20-20 eyesight, long-held positions with the firm and the accompanying prestige and meaning for us, long-held ideas, or points of view.

But if this is dying, it also adds up to the exotic movement we call living. It is also part of the miracle of growing. Whoever heard of a story that stood still, a game in which the score never changed, or a play in which no one ever entered or exited the stage?

Part of the secret of a fear-surpassing life is to live *within* each moment, rather than being simply a window-shopper or skeptical passerby.

Lady Bird Johnson, following the death of her husband, said she had now put her thoughts into two categories: the "Aren't-you-glad-thats" and "If-onlys."

"We should think about the first column ahead of time and savor things more when we have them," she said. "To be close to death gives you a new awareness of the preciousness of life, and the extreme tenuousness of it. You must live every day to the fullest, as though you had a short supply— because you do. I said that glibly for years, but I didn't know how intensely one should live."

Jimmy Carter was asked by reporters if the night he won the presidential election would go down as the happiest moment of his life.

"No," he answered without needing time to think it over.

"Which, then?" they wanted to know.

He told about the night the Carters' daughter, Amy, had been born. He and his sons, the youngest then fifteen, were so excited they woke up all their friends in Plains, Georgia, at two o'clock in the morning to tell them the news.

Emily Dickinson, the Belle of Amherst, gives us another sample of splendor in the opening lines of her poem about sunrise:

I'll tell you how the Sun rose—
A Ribbon at a time—
The Steeples swam in Amethyst—
The news, like Squirrels, ran—
The Hills untied their Bonnets—
The Bobolinks—begun—
Then I said softly to myself—
"That must have been the Sun"!

Sunrises, though, are matched by sunsets. Events shake our houses of life, and we have no choice but to decide whether to live in the new world that has suddenly asserted itself and included us, or to run in fear's direction.

Under discussion in a 1977 Rose Bowl pregame interview was Michigan coach Bo Schembechler's heart attack of a few years before, which had been followed by openheart surgery—a development some held had resulted in a noticeable change in the sort of person Mr. Schembechler seemed to be. A sports publicity director from the university agreed with this speculation that, yes, he was a different man than before the surgery.

"As an English professor once told me," said the director, "some time in life, every adult will have a great experience that will change him."

Crossroad moments can be represented by the seemingly mysterious intervention of God or experience of God's presence, a life-changing friendship, a bereavement, a falling in love, failure, or, as with Coach Schembechler, healing from an illness.

And faith has the proven ability to make us more than conquerors.

"In everything," wrote Paul, "God is at work for good . . ."

We will, of course, go on worrying and wondering.

In bed on sleepless nights, disconcerting little scenarios may be acted out in our heads. We want to trust God, the flow of events, and our own resourcefulness, but this may be hard to do if bills lie on the desk unpaid, if nothing seems to work in trying to deal with an overweight problem, if the doctor acknowledged that he isn't quite sure what is wrong, or if depression persists and nothing seems to be happening to lift that irrational veil of gloom.

We sit in church and listen to promises of companionship and strength, of eventual reunions, yet find death hard to think about, and harder still to talk about.

The only contingencies, though, that we need honestly to fear, and the only perishings without a rebuttal are those that kill our inward dream, that stamp out our belief that God is for us, that on a scale of one to ten, we matter infinitely both to God and to one another.

We cannot let ourselves see ourselves as victims or as the prisoners of the expectations of others. Thus we will not only practice the skills of release; we will also practice testing the radical authority and potentials of love.

We may fail. We *know* we will die. Little matter. The issue is not that. It is our determination to live in the spirit of William Carey of India whose motto was: "Expect great things *from* God; attempt great things *for* God."

Here, then, is the fear that fears only one thing: that life will be missed, its magnificence go unrecognized, its tender hours be left unused.

It sounds trite, even philosophically shopworn, to advocate that we live one day at a time. Yet that may be one of the most important things God is trying to say to us by the way life is arranged.

A generation ago a motto was placed above fireplace mantles in many homes. It read simply:

> Fear knocked at the door,
> Faith answered.
> There was no one there.

Our Understandable
Disinterest
in Dying

When the disciples caught sight of [Jesus] walking on
the water they were terrified. "It's a ghost!" they said,
and screamed with fear.

But at once Jesus spoke to them. "It's all right! It's I
myself, don't be afraid!"

(Matt. 14:26-27 Phillips)

Death is different from every other human
experience. We find that out early.

A young mother died. The night before the
funeral the bereft father took his three children
with him to the chapel for a few final moments
together.

Looking down into the casket from a perch on her
father's shoulder, three-year-old, blue-eyed Marilyn
asked, "Can she wiggle?"

We see death in flowers, civilization, animals, and
the sadness of fall.

We know marriages die. That corporations go
kaput. That seasons leave. That stars burn up.

There is a principle of perishability in the bosom of things.

The deaths of persons, though, remain mentally staggering events to which we never become more than only partially reconciled, and *faith* meets its severest test of all when the words must be spoken, however compassionately, "I'm sorry, but he's gone."

Or, we say of ninety-one-year-old Mrs. B., who is *non compos mentis*, that she has outlived all her friends and survives on baby food, and that "her death can only be a blessing." Yet, beneath that exterior of decay is a uniquely beautiful human being—a nonrepeatable combination of genes and dreams, of tears and involvements—kisses, eyes, hair, hands, prayers, laughter, heartbeats, parties, snowflakes against the face, bus rides, breakfasts, budgets, and benedictions.

Death confronts us with the "irretrievable."

With most developments in our lives we can, if we lose, regroup, turn, and stand to fight again. We can fix up, trade off, apologize, correct, wait-and-see, hope, save our money, do fifty other things to position us for another shot at the future. But death draws a double line under our names. Account closed.

In Utah there's a small university called Weber State. It emerges out of relative obscurity each year as a result of its fine basketball teams. I'm sure it's not so obscure for people who live nearby, or to its alumni, but it may seem so in metropolitan areas. The newspaper story, though, did not concern

Weber State's basketball team, but its choir. It was on a tour of California with a scheduled singing stop in San Francisco. For some it was a first visit to the Coast and their first look at the Pacific Ocean.

When the bus driver made a brief relaxation stop at a Bay area beach the students got out and dabbled in the surf. They didn't know the tides could be treacherous, and in a few terrifying moments two young men students, both twenty-one, wound up being swept by its power into the sea. Suddenly the tour was over for them—the tour of life.

I've only seen one person actually die, though I've waited and prayed beside hundreds of bedsides where life was rapidly slipping away.

Mr. Thompson's departure was different.

His wife called late one afternoon. She said it looked like Mr. T. wouldn't live through the night, that he was being allowed to die at home as he had requested. But she was alone, and could I come by and spend a few moments with her before dark?

As I entered the bedroom, Mr. Thompson was breathing heavily, his eyelids closed.

I took one of his hands in one of mine and hers in the other, then after about five minutes of just being quiet and thankful there together, I said the twenty-third Psalm.

Another five minutes went by, gradually his breathing slowed, then completely stopped. We looked at each other—exchanging the peace that surpasses understanding.

I went to the telephone and dialed.

Yet, in spite of the blow death deals our sensibilities, it seems to be, in its own way, as correct as life.

The universe would be an empty affair without life—a gala without guests; a world all dressed up with nothing to do, nowhere to go. But without death, life would stop being life.

Someone has said that God could cure us of our distaste of death by requiring everyone to live at least three hundred years!

Death also loses its power to nail us to the wall of fear if we learn to appreciate that it is not the worst thing that can happen to anyone, no matter what is said.

We won't waste time trying to imagine what the "worst" might be, but I like what G. A. Studdert-Kennedy told his small son when he went off to war. He asked him to pray that God would "make Daddy brave." It would be all right, he said, for the boy to pray for his father's safe return, but he didn't want that to be the first request.

"Daddy dead," he told him, "would be Daddy still. Daddy dishonored would be another matter."

When we must do business with death, we have to let ourselves feel the awfulness, the awesomeness of it. Let it burn, hurt, crush us.

At the same time, lay alongside that crucifying reality two other realities: gratitude and hope.

Plus the belief that God is there—crying, loving, hurting, caring beside us.

The ultimate death remains at 100 percent. Thus the question is not whether we shall die, or who shall die, but how we shall choose to live.

Most of us would, no doubt, choose a long life in preference to a short one, given the chance, but quality is more decisive than quantity. Methuselah lived 969 years. Whether his life made any difference to anyone we do not know.

And coming to terms with death—locating it inside, not outside of the wisdom of God, is to enter the house of Easter.

Easter involves an up-and-over-the-Empire-State-Building bound by the mind and soul. It is a voyage by faith—out beyond the two-hundred mile limits of what we can prove logically or scientifically.

In a feature story on Irving Wallace, an interviewer said of him: "He lives the way a larger-than-life novelist should. Between books he travels abroad, frequently to Venice or Paris, recharging his psyche with the electricity of new vistas."

The same recharging possibility is open for us—even without a long overseas flight, if we catch a vision of what Easter-life living is about—if we practice living abundantly, compassionately, radically, wonderfully, appreciatively each day.

Philip J. Bailey reminds us that:

> We live in deeds, not years; in thought,
>   not breath;
> In feelings, not in figures on a dial.
> We should count time by heart-throbs.

It isn't that we are afraid of those last fifteen minutes of life. Rather it's the fear that *neither* death nor life have any abiding significance that gets to us.

Whether we think of death as a built-in process that is intrinsic and necessary to a growing, changing universe, or as an enemy whose power has been broken by Jesus Christ, we find in Christianity the offer of a place to stand, a Love in which to believe, a victory to win, a way to overcome the fear of extinction.

Death isn't sleep. Nor is heaven a big pink and blue playground where no one has to work, where there is no more developing to do. It's a place for push-ups and high adventure. Death is the price and prerequisite of something wonderful, as right for itself as this world of time and perishable materials is right for itself.

The death question forces us into a showdown with ourselves about God—makes us ask whether talk of God and resurrection is real or imaginary.

Is Easter the wish-projection of cowards—something manufactured to ease the pain of death's permanency? Or is it what journalists call "hard news" about the human situation?

Is it a tongue-in-cheek ritual we engage in good-naturedly with a "maybe-there-is-something" attitude, or, after the laughter of our St. Peter-pearly gates jokes fades away, the end of kidding?

That's something each of us must decide. Saying yes to Easter doesn't mean we possess explanations that are altogether satisfying intellectually, or that, having come down on the side of yes, we no longer wonder and worry about dying—that we no longer grieve, no longer struggle with granitelike truth.

What it does mean is that we've decided not to play God. We allow God to be God so we can be our own non-god selves, can trade in exhausting anxieties for freedom.

We are heartened by the fantastic renaissance of the land after the winter freeze. Equally are we uplifted by the testimony of the Crucified who rejoins his friends on the Emmaus Road, and who, in the stillness of a garden, says a girl's name.

I've just put down the Los Angeles *Times* where I read how the eighteen-year-old son of a professional football coach of the Rams was seated in the car of one of his friends at an intersection in Long Beach. As they waited for the traffic light to change, a drunken driver plowed into the two boys broadside, killing the coach's son and critically injuring his friend.

We twist logic out of shape if we take heartbreak such as that and write beneath it, "This is what God intended for that young man."

It is more difficult to take the position that many sorts of adversity and suffering must remain unexplained. But that's better for coping than adopting distorted interpretations of divine judgment such as the ones Job's friends offered him. It also leaves the way open for maximizing the possibilities of creative endurance and triumphant courage.

To say we do not have answers is not to say we have nothing.

What we have is hope, one another, and a powerful Promise.

We do not know what the future holds. We do think we know Who holds the future.

I remember the Easter morning when I was twelve. As part of the sunrise service I was scheduled to read a poem. I wore a new pair of white shoes for the occasion, and worship at sunup—well, that's bound to be exciting. But it rained. Rain came down in silver sheets, and the service had to be held inside the church building with the lights on.

But the poem lingers. It was Kipling's—where he sees all of us in heaven with palette and brush and painter's smock, dabbing away at the details of paradise:

> When Earth's last picture is painted and the tubes are
> twisted and dried,
> When the oldest colours have faded, and the
> youngest critic has died,
> We shall rest, and, faith, we shall need it—lie down
> for an aeon or two,
> Till the Master of All Good Workmen shall put us to
> work anew.
> And those that were good shall be happy: they shall
> sit in a golden chair;
> They shall splash at a ten-league canvas with brushes
> of comets' hair.
> They shall find real saints to draw from—Magdalene,
> Peter, and Paul;

They shall work for an age at a sitting and never be
    tired at all!
And only The Master shall praise us, and only The
    Master shall blame;
And no one shall work for money, and no one shall
    work for fame,
But each for the joy of the working, and each, in his
    separate star,
Shall draw the Thing as he sees It for the God of
    Things as They are!

Learning to die is learning to live.

We can live our dying—face it, accept it, revel in it as mystery, allow it to teach us the wonder of each day, the fragile sparkle of each fleeting second.

Death is as wise as God, as much a part of the totality of things as the light of Venus in the western sky at ten o'clock on a summer night. But its beauty and deeper purpose remain a secret until we meet the Christ, and, when we do that, fear is under orders to untie us and let us go.

Some Techniques
of Fear
Management

God hath not given us the spirit of fear;
but of power, and of love, and of a sound mind.
(II Tim. 1:7 KJV)

In the first pages of this book we talked about signs
that trigger our minds into fresh forms of mental
activity.

A favorite I like to recall is one I saw along a New
York thruway. The road ahead was narrowing and
the sign said: "Squeeze Left." "Soft Shoulders" also
makes us smile. And ministers who would like to
see their churches filled on Sundays envy the
cleverness of the got-there-first commercial that
reads: "Weekends Were Made for Michelob."

Another sign we often see reads: "Under New
Management." If we can allow ourselves to apply
that kind of announcement to fear, we will come
close to appreciating what the next few pages are
intended to be about.

What are some solid techniques for bringing fear

under new management? I'd like to take us from *logos* to *praxis*, from wordy theories to a few commonsense suggestions that can help us live life with less fear and more joy—maybe as soon as tomorrow!

Here's my Rx:

1. It helps to know that everyone, at times, is afraid. We would be subhuman or antihuman if we lacked the capacity to be afraid.

2. It also helps us to become emotionally competent if we can learn to speak plainly about experiences that involve pain, if we will name things for what they are. "Then Jesus told them plainly, 'Lazarus is dead'" (John 11:14).

3. It helps to accept the fact that everyone doesn't like us. We would be moral zeroes if they did.

4. Life is fragile, not necessarily fair. It's also drenched in change. It wouldn't be as beautiful, and not nearly so important, if God had made it otherwise. That isn't an easy admission to make. But, if we can make it, fear will begin to take a back seat.

5. When things don't work out in ways that seem correct or desirable to us, they often wind up leading us down new, previously unimagined roads which turn out to be as good as they are surprising. Failures and defeats are not as final as they seem.

6. A wise prayer says, "God, help me handle my possessions with a light touch." Losses aren't as frightening, nor is the threat of losses, if we can find a way to live up to the spirit of that plea.

7. Final judgments or permanent choices shouldn't be made at 3:00 A.M., or at times when we are tired. Fear tends to have its best innings in such moments. To rule out the necessity of making decisions under those adverse kinds of circumstances is to counterattack.

8. We can discount by 90 percent those doom warnings that have flooded public conversation ever since we first learned to speak and write. A few of them deserve analysis and response. Most are but bizarre bids for attention.

9. We help to hold fear in check if we refuse to require perfection of ourselves, if we believe once in a while it's okay to fall on our faces or break our necks. We become unctuous and separate from mankind if we have no room in our value system for such things to happen to us.

10. Nor should we attempt to play God or take responsibility for the whole world. That's a quick way to turn into a blithering idiot, of becoming part of the problem rather than part of the answer.

Lying beyond these somewhat oversimplified "rules of thumb" is, of course, a vast world of research and psychological information having to do with fear—both fear that is pathological and fear that falls within the parameters of normal human functioning.

The central premise most behavioral scientists use is that nearly all fears are learned responses, and that, by following known steps, fear can be unlearned.

Treatment usually consists of a candid and intensive analysis of what it is that makes us afraid, utilizing notebooks and *lists* of fear-inducing objects and situations—breaking down experience into smaller units. Then follows emotional reconditioning, a *systematic desensitization* utilizing both fantasy and reality. Cerebral calisthenics.

If, for example, someone is terrified at the thought of flying in a plane, the whole process of mentally visualizing the trip, consulting printed matter on how the plane functions, driving to the terminal, buying the ticket, boarding, buckling up, taking off, listening for the thump of wheels locking into place is all cataloged and rehearsed. First in imagination. Later, through gradually increased stages of reality.

The mind is taught to function as a control tower, giving calming captain's instructions. Relaxation helps the body accept the mind's orders, and, eventually a new set of responses takes over.

There's no denying the value of this learning-in-reverse. But *spiritual resources* are also significant assets in the search for composure in the face of threatening situations.

Here are a few we may want to try to make our own:

Active Love. Love is spiritual energy, particularly if it is understood as something more than natural and spontaneous emotion. Love can be deliberate, run counter to natural feeling. It is a mighty weapon against the unknown, *a theology of meaning.* All of us are theologians of one kind or another. When our theology is honest and we are more interested in truth than in being defensive about our own goodness, we become less frightened. Faith, we need to remember, continues to be faith; it is not biblical argument.

Community. We can't be human alone, and we can't learn to know God well unless we allow ourselves to become part of some mutually supportive fellowship that is concerned about the imperishables. Fear will not altogether leave us, but neither will it master us if we have the support of friends who are ready to act on our behalf and affirm us as persons of worth.

Conversation. Talking troubles over with someone we trust usually calms us down and helps us get things in perspective. We are reminded that the sun will come up again tomorrow, that death is part of life, that there will be a way, that failures are not final, that "in everything" God is at work for good. Fear gains on us only when we stop asking questions.

Prayer. Prayer is the ground floor. It is an artesian spring, generating new courage within us, because it is the surest testimony we have that we are not the pawns of fate but beloved children of God.

If our inner worlds are thus fed, the space left for nagging, destructive, happiness-stealing fears will be small.

Let's say it once more; it will help make us strong if we admit that we *are* afraid in certain circumstances, not all of them logical or legitimate. We can make that acknowledgment and know that we are human beings.

Pablo Casals said, "The main thing in life is not to be afraid to be human."

So if getting up in front of a crowd to speak or perform gives you rubber legs, join the club. If staying alone in the house at night gives you the willies, that's not so crazy either. All loneliness carries a few coattail fears along with it.

But when fear produces excessive perspiration or a racing heart, we need to hear: "In quietness and in trust shall be your strength." "Be still, and know that I am God" (Isa. 30:15; Ps. 46:10). We will experience hurt, become nervous or nauseous, suffer other kinds of emotional distress, but we will not cop out.

We may allow ourselves other options—laughing, crying, blushing, or falling down. But we will not flee.

If strangers scare us, or confrontations with people who dislike us cause us to shiver, at least we will put ourselves in their presence. If we cannot speak their names aloud or start a conversation, we will try to smile.

If the thought of riding an elevator to the thirtieth floor of an office building causes us to come apart at the seams, we will still go, taking someone with us, practicing on smaller buildings ahead of time.

But we won't settle for defeat.

We will try to open up the doors and the windows of our souls and let in sunshine, wind, and rain to help us grow into greater psychic durability.

We will walk, travel, touch, listen to music, ask questions, go to the movies and to church, read novels, and write friends. We will attend weddings and funerals. Explore the Bible, pray the best we can. We will dress interestingly, learn to enjoy interruptions, do things that make us tired. We will paint something, plant something, create something. We will correspond with our senator or someone who lives in another country, become interested in our local team, call someone on the phone, enjoy the funnies, read a best seller.

Mental and emotional illness doesn't occur all at once. More often it is the result of an extended accumulation of distortions. Mental health is also accumulative, the sum of dozens of life-renewing, happiness-reclaiming moments.

We will make use of our "little dyings" as part of heaven's extension curriculum.

And we'll remember what Br'er Fox said to Peter Rabbit: "You can't run away from trouble. There ain't no place that far!"

The thing all fear has in common is the thought of losing something: our poise, our health, a member of our family through sickness or an accident, our tomorrows. Yet there is no life without losing. None at all. Unless one day ends, another cannot begin. Unless childhood yields, no one would ever grow up.

Trust can outfight, outlast fear. And there is nothing wrong with being extravagant with love.

If someone cherished is taken from us, our love for

that person remains valid. That is something we will always own.

If a social situation frightens us, we will vow to remember that other people—and these persons in particular—were created by God for love. Their yearnings and anxieties are as great, if not greater, than our own.

And, if we are distraught by the thought we might fail at something, we can ponder the victory of the cross.

Love is trust practicing its profession. It's the finding that replaces losing.

Here, then, are some of our stops on the road to the City of Peace:

* Affirm yourself and own up to your capacity to be afraid.

* Settle this: you will not run. You will not always be able to stand erect or be satisfied with your performances, but you will stay and fight.

* Fill your emotional cup with all the good things you can, leaving minimum room for fear.

* Take an appropriate amount of responsibility for your life—for your behavior, your safety, your capacity to be adequate. But don't take it all. God didn't create you in the image of total sufficiency. God would be disappointed if you bought into such an illusion.

* Love. Endlessly and passionately. Forgive and care. Love trades one kind of control for another.

James Maloney, who spent the first years of his life in California, died in Ohio. He and his wife, Lois, were members of a church in Akron, and when Jim died at age fifty-eight after losing his fight against cancer, Lois and the Maloney's three sons brought his body west for burial.

Through a friend I was asked to take charge of a memorial service.

Jim had been captain of the *Columbia*, the big blimp we see hovering over football games, parades, historical events of various kinds. And the big ship and its new crew were on hand as the family gathered on a green Covina hillside for the committal.

A hundred of us surrounded the grave as I read from the Old and New Testaments, the *Columbia* hovering three or four miles away in radio contact with one of Jim's fellow officers who stood beside the Maloney family.

The reading finished, I asked everyone to bow for final prayers of thanksgiving.

Our heads tilted forward, we began to hear the approach of the blimp.

As a hot sun warmed the napes of our necks, my prayer found its ending in the words of First Corinthians: "Love knows no limit of its endurance."

The throb of engines grew louder. The *Columbia* is coming!

"No end to its trust; no fading of its hope; it can outlast anything . . ."

Now it was directly over us—no more than fifty feet and almost touchable as we discovered when the amen had been said and we raised our heads and eyes.

Exhilarated by the experience, we found ourselves looking into the faces of the flight team.

The flowers, tossed by the crew, began to drift down from the massive silver bullet, color spattering the dirt mound and the heads and shoulders of the crowd. Roses. Carnations. And jonquils.

We waved. The Maloneys, too, raised their hands and smiled.

Peace rained, and reigned.

Then, pivoted on a dime-sized point, the nose of the *Columbia* was pointed straight upward. Within moments it disappeared—into a covering of California haze.

We meet God in glimpses.

There are times when God seems out of reach. Or we allow ourselves to grow out of touch with God. God hovers there—the final Reality, the Alpha and Omega, the Truth about everything—the Love that will not let us go, that will not let us down, and that will not let us off.

There may be a roar of engines. Or only Splendid Quiet. Perhaps a set of blue-green eyes looking into our own. Then, somehow the Living Christ is there, making his way into our lives to soften sorrow, relax tension, cause fear to dissolve in a photosynthesis of grace.

A Nest
Among the Stars

I will build me a nest on the greatness of God.
—Sidney Lanier

You probably never have heard of John Stavast.
Unless you are Shirley, his wife, or his parents. Or
that air force official, who, in the mid-sixties, had the
responsibility of notifying John's family that he had
been shot down and taken prisoner by the North
Vietnamese. Or, on an outside chance, you were in
our Claremont congregation that Sunday, six and a
half years later, when he walked down the center
aisle—handsome, gentle, clear-eyed—and reported
to the four hundred of us there—those of us who had
prayed for him during those years—that faith still
overcomes the world.

He spoke to us that day about how he had looked
through the door of the prison blockhouse one
night—a door left ajar by a negligent guard—and
watched a full moon ascend the eastern sky. He said
he knew that same light looked down upon the

United States, and that the sphere that spanned those distances both of miles and ideologies was emblematic of a love that did the same.

"Though we were far apart," he said, "that bit of moon shining through the doorway brought me huge comfort, and my prayers never stopped."

Like most pilots, John Stavast has been more at home in the sky than on the ground.

Thus, it was no surprise when, to show his appreciation to a community of believers that had maintained a vigil for him and never surrendered hope, he presented to the church a Franklin Mint bronze eagle mounted on a base that carried his and Shirley's names and this reference to the words of Isaiah the prophet:

> They who wait for the Lord shall renew their strength, they shall mount up with wings like eagles, they shall run and not be weary, they shall walk and not faint. (40:31)

There is such a thing as the Eagle Life. And whoever knows about it is bound to know some of the strategies of triumph over fear.

It is the life of maximums, not minimums, of running more than rest—the life of the open hand rather than the tight fist, of waiting as well as of working.

Franklin Roosevelt, the American president who challenged the nation to defuse its fear as it floundered in the financial depression of the early thirties, and said that all we have really to fear is fear itself, experienced considerable anxiety when all four of his sons wound up in posts of danger during World War II. Eleanor Roosevelt is reported to have said to him then, "You mustn't bring up your children like eagles and expect them to act like sparrows."

Our retrospect on Vietnam gives her statement another meaning now, but the point was plain then.

The eagle is a big bird, an easy mark for a gun. Wing spans reach up to ten feet. Speeds: as great as twenty-four miles an hour. Altitudes: over a mile above earth.

Most of the time we don't feel like eagles. More like robins with broken wings, we want the sky, but settle for a grubbing for worms.

The Bible tells of several eagle personalities, and Obadiah may have been one. He was a young man who spoke out against the arrogance of Edom, a country which appeared to be delighted by the sack of its neighbor, Judah, in 586 B.C. Thousands of Jerusalem citizens were hauled off as Babylonian slaves.

Obadiah warned Edom that her glee would be brief.

"Though you soar aloft like the eagle, though your nest is set among the stars . . . [God] will bring you down" (Obad. 1:4, italics mine).

Though these words are in the form of a warning, I want to use them as descriptive of what it means for us to live lives of boldness and spiritual risk.

Faith in God provides us with a nest of confidence, a refuge and launch site interestingly suspended between the business of earth and the promise of heaven. It is a fragile nest of hope, not an armor-plated fortress of doctrine, but it protects us against a philosophy of absolute zero and life-denying cynicism. It puts us up among soul country where the wind currents are strong, where only the daring venture.

But we have difficulty letting go and letting God. We want to make faith fact. We ask for an iron-clad guarantee, forgetting Kirsopp Lake's definition that "faith is not belief in spite of evidence but life in scorn of confidence."

Faith finds its security in the flight, not in the airport, and we are made for lofty elevations.

Sidney Lanier, looking out over marsh country near St. Simons Island, Georgia, wrote:

As the marsh-hen secretly builds on the watery sod,
Behold I will build me a nest on the greatness of God.

Modern geology has concluded that we are "star children"—literally so. The earth, so science now says, has been formed by combinations or coalescences of old stars which once experienced their own births, aged, then died in debris-scattering explosions so colossal that to describe them as a series of compounded Fourths of July would be like comparing the Pacific to a fishpond.

We are made, not of dust, but of *stardust*.

123

Christian faith arms us against panic by reminding us that, while we're part of a frolic of atoms—the ceaseless swirl of a ceaseless creation—we're more than assorted biological pieces of a puzzle.

One December, fire broke out in the San Gabriel mountains which surround the beautiful Southern California valley in which I live. Arriving home at six o'clock that evening from work and turning into Queens Court, I was suddenly aware that the whole town was becoming ringed by flames. The fire apparently had been raging throughout the day—"up in the hills," we said. There had been smoke, but it was mixed with clouds. Now, darkness provided the contrast which helped me see how close the fires had spread.

As I entered the house I saw my wife and daughter making cookies and talking over the day's events.

"How can you be so unconcerned?" I thought, as I burst into the kitchen. "Haven't you been outside?" I asked, my face and voice full of alarm.

We rushed into the street. In the darkness the flames looked like the end of time. We prepared to water down the roof, called our neighbors.

Eventually the fires were controlled. And miraculously, no lives were lost, though parts of the mountainsides will be black for years.

It's an old saying that "we would never have seen the stars if the night had not come." And we could say the same thing about fear. We wouldn't have realized how close the fires were without the dark. Just so fear lights up another landscape. It arouses the body, sets it for action. It calls up reserve armies, enables us to know what prizes are at stake and how important it is not to defer our response. It gives us the competitor's edge. It says "do something!"

Fear, in reasonable amounts and at appropriate times, is an asset. It is part of our defense system, determined to protect boundaries.

In Herman Melville's *Moby Dick* the first mate, Starbuck, is described as a man of outstanding courage. He is also the one who said, "I will have no man in my boat who is not afraid of a whale."

The fear of becoming careless while driving a car or flying a plane, of failing an examination, or of coming across with a shoddy performance as an entertainer may improve our chances of safe and successful outcome. The border, though, between positive fear and the negative overwhelming fear that wrecks our sanity is narrow and hard to locate, which may simply be reminder number forty-seven that we were not designed as small tin gods but as limited expressions of God's neatest idea.

And if the stars are mortal like ourselves they nevertheless outshine our mistakes. They symbolize those out-of-reach realities to which we still hitch wagons.

God is our hope. Even when we're stubborn, cruel, wallowing in materialistic excesses, broken in half by the consequences of conceit and self-centeredness, or mesmerized by our fears, God doesn't give up on our eagle possibilities.

We write about a post-Christian world and the end

of faith. We eat the bread of affluence and stay hungry. And in the midst of data processing, cities that fly, and budgets in billions, there's still in our throats that song the brokenhearted African father sings in the musical play *Lost in the Stars* by Kurt Weill and Maxwell Anderson (based on Alan Paton's book *Cry, the Beloved Country*):

> And sometimes it seems maybe God's gone away
> And we're lost out there in the stars.

This is the primal worry, the cosmic fear. That there is no God, that nothing really abides, nothing finally counts. We flounder in tangles of a mystery we can't comprehend. We look for certainties, find only rocks and air and no one there.

Then it's Christmas Eve, or Easter morning, and faith brings its magic show back to town. We're lifted out of a preoccupation with the six o'clock news by Handel's *Messiah*. Our sense of wonder returns. We pause to remember how much we love one another and it begins to dawn on us, as it did upon John Stavast, that these are mirrors of another love that created and is still creating something as beautiful as it is brave—that (though it's a somewhat embarrassing admission to make) we have spent a lot of time looking for God in a lot of wrong places.

Because of Christ we have a nest among the stars, a home for our hearts. It's a fragile basket, made of manger straw and the mud of ordinary days. But somewhere, out there in the shining distance, we know the *Columbia* is coming!

And we will go on living with these fears of ours—valuing some, rejecting others, knowing that faith, hope, and love, for those who dare to trust in them, are Lights of victory.

They are the first stars of evening, and the last to fade away as the drama of a new day begins.

PRESCRIPTION FOR PEACE

Strike a balance between work and play, between seriousness and laughter. Go to church regularly. Also to the ball game.

Stick with the truth even if it makes you look or feel bad. Falsehoods are wandering ghosts.

Forgive your enemies as part of the price you pay for the privilege of being forgiven. Realize that you are sometimes a "pain in the neck" yourself.

Walk. Get lots of air and sunshine. Occasionally some rain or snow in your face; some dirt on your hands.

Talk your troubles over with someone you trust. Your dreams, too.

Don't underestimate the ability of God to straighten out a situation, even when you can't. And give God a little time.

Discriminate among your fears. Learn to tell which ones are useful, which ones destructive.

Remember that the ultimate death rate is still 100 percent. You would be getting "gypped" if everyone got to die and you didn't.

When you can't sleep, say: "Aha! Here's a chance for a little privacy and creative thinking. All day long I've been too busy to pray; now I can get around to thanking God."

Fall in love with life, with children, older people, sports cars, the theater, music, books, cities, hills, the Bible, everything except money.